SMALL SPACES

Stylish Ideas

for Making

More of Less

in the Home

SMALL

SPACES

Stylish Ideas
for Making
More of Less
in the Home

By Azby Brown

Photographs by Yoshio Shiratori

KODANSHA INTERNATIONAL

TOKYO ❑ NEW YORK ❑ LONDON

Distributed in the United States by Kodansha America, Inc., 114 Fifth Avenue, New York, N.Y., 10011, and in the United Kingdom and continental Europe by Kodansha Europe Ltd., Gillingham House, 38–44 Gillingham Street, London, SW1V 1HU. Published by Kodansha International Ltd., 17–14 Otowa 1-chome, Bunkyo-ku, Tokyo 112, and Kodansha America, Inc.

Printed in Japan. First edition, 1993.
93 94 95 96   10 9 8 7 6 5 4 3 2 1

Library of Congress Cataloging in Publication Data
Brown, Azby, 1956-
    Smallspace: stylish ideas for making more of less in the home/
text and illustrations by Azby Brown: photographs by Yoshio
Shiratori.
    1. Interior decoration—Japan—Human factors.
    2. Personal space—psychological aspects. I, Title.
NK2084.A1B76 1993
    728',37'0952—dc20   82-36529
                                                              CIP

ISBN 4–7700–1495–3

PAGE 2: Detail of house in Narashino. Designer: Shoroku Tsukuda. Photo by Yoshio Shiratori. (See page 7).

COVER: Second floor loft intended as child's room. Designer: Atelier Mobile. Photo by Yoshio Shiratori (See page 87)

ACKNOWLEDGMENTS

The author wishes to thank all who assisted in the realization of this book: the homeowners, designers, journalists, and friends who called ideas to my attention and made time in their busy schedules to accommodate what were usually very nosy investigations. Particular thanks in this regard is due Mr. Tsuneo Shimojima of Pittori Piccoli who has been particularly generous with his time and engaging in his dialogue, and who shares my "passion for the relevatory mundane." Thanks, of course, to Yoshio Shiratori, a photographer who truly possesses architectural vision, and Dana Levy, a designer who seems to have magically found room for everything on the page. Finally, the editors, Barry Lancet for his well-targeted "point-sharpening" and Michiko Uchiyama for her endless, tireless, complaint-free, and enthusiastic help with research, contacts, appointments, reminders, and health advice.

ARCHITECTS/DESIGNERS: Tsutomu Abe (14), (15); p. 33, fig. 5; p. 88, fig. 8 ● Amorphe Associates (55); p. 83, fig. 6 ● Tadao Ando (4) , (5); p. 13, fig. 1 ● Harumi Asano p. 88, fig. 6 ● Atelier Mobile, front jacket, (10), (11), (57); p. 25, fig. 1; p. 87, fig. 3 ● Takamitsu and Rie Azuma (21); p. 45, fig. 1 ● Cozy Living Co., Ltd p. 52, fig. 6 ● Akira Fujii p. 28, fig. 2 ● Masao Hayakawa p. 58, fig. 13 ● Kenji Hongo (26), (27); p. 51, figs. 3 & 4 ● Kazumichi Iimura p. 52, fig. 9 ● Keiichi Irie p. 77, fig. 1 ● Ben Ishii (Time Architects) (20) ● Jun Itami (8), (9); p. 21, fig. 1 ● Toyoo Ito (18), (19); p. 16, fig. 2; p. 41, fig. 4 ● Shigeko Kato (22), (23) ; p. 46, fig. 2 ● Kenji Kawabata p. 41, fig. 3 ● Mariko Kimura, back jacket (bottom right), (56); p. 85, fig. 1; p. 86, fig. 2 ● Hisao Koyama p. 33, fig. 4 ● Masayuki Kurokawa p. 69, fig. 2 ● Hiroo Maruya p. 24, figs. 3 & 4; p. 57, figs. 7 & 8; p. 88, fig. 5 & 7 ● Mamoru Misawa and Kengaku Architects & Engineering Inc. p. 48, fig. 7 ● Tsunekata Naito p. 36, fig. 6 ● Pittori Piccoli Inc., back jacket (left), (6), (7), (24), (25), (28-32), (35-50), (58); p. 17, fig. 1; p. 20, figs. 2-4; p. 49, fig. 1; p. 50, fig. 2; p. 53, fig. 1; p. 55, figs. 2 & 3; p. 56, figs. 4 & 6; p. 66, fig. 8; p. 68, fig. 9; p. 69, fig. 1; p. 70, figs. 3 & 4; p. 72, fig. 5; p. 73, fig. 1; p. 76, fig. 2; p. 88, fig. 4 ● Kazuyo Sejima p. 84, fig. 11 ● Shimizu Corporation, Design Division (12), (13); p. 29, fig. 1; p. 32, fig. 2 ● Tsuneo Shimojima (Pittori Piccoli Inc.) (52), (53); p. 80, fig. 3 ● Ichiro Toda (16), (17); p. 37, fig. 1 ● Shoroku Tsukuda, back jacket (bottom left), (1) ● Ushida-Findlay Partnership, back jacket (top right), (2), (51), (54); p. 10, fig. 8; p. 78, fig. 2; p. 82, fig. 5; p. 96, fig. 9 ● Akira Yamada (33), (34); p. 61, figs. 1-3 ● Shoei Yo (3).

PHOTO CREDITS: Susumu Koshimizu (pl. 20), Osamu Murai (pls. 8 & 9), Tomio Ohashi (pl. 19), Shigeru Ono (pl. 18), Pittori Piccoli Inc. (pls. 28-32, 35-41, 44-50, and 58), Project 90 (pl. 55).

FOR PERMISSION TO PHOTOGRAPH: Toshiaki Chine, Veronique Henry, Hosaka Animal Clinic, Kyozo Iinuma, Hideto Isoda, Takayasu and Hiromi Iwamoto, Tatsuo Kawaguchi, Reiko Kawamura, MCH Jukukan Research Institute, Yoko Mori, Masakatsu Murata, Yuji Ono, Koji and Konomi Oshima, Tsuneo Shimojima.

FOR GENERAL ASSISTANCE: Inax Corporation, Matsushita Electric Works, Mariko Nishioka, Pittori Piccoli Inc., Sanwa Shutter Corporation, Sekisui Chemical Co., Ltd., YKK Architectural Products Inc.

FOR PERMISSION TO USE EXISTING MATERIAL: Yoshihiko Ando, Tokumasa Ariyama, Tetsuo Hida, Tamotsu Miyamoto, Iwao Nakamura, Hiroaki Okuma, Norifumi Onishi, Takashi Shinomiya, Akihiko Shishikura, Kazuomi Yoshida.

ILLUSTRATION CREDITS: The following illustrations were adapted and redrawn for this book: figs. 3 & 4 on p. 24, fig. 6 on p. 36, figs. 7 & 8 on p. 57, figs. 5 & 7 on p. 88 from "Sumai no aidia sukecchi shu" by Hiroo Maruya ©1984, Shokokusha Publishing Co., Ltd; fig. 6 on p. 88 from "Sukusuku Nobinobi Kodomobeya" by MAG Kenchiku Sekkei group © 1988, Economic Research Association; fig. 13 on p. 58 from "Jutaku Kenchiku," January 1989, p. 41, published by Kenchiku Shiryo Kenkyusha, photography by Shigeo Okamoto; fig. 2 on p. 28 (July 1989, p. 62), fig. 7 on p. 48 (March 1989, p. 128), fig. 9 on p. 52 (March 1989), fig. 8 on p. 88 (October 1989, p. 64) from "JA House" published from Shinkenchiku-sha Co., Ltd.

Contents

COMPACT, COMFORTABLE, CONVENIENT

Home is where the heart is. Our homes become part of us, shape us, and reflect our desires and habits to a far greater degree than most of us realize. And despite the potential pleasure our homes can provide, few people are satisfied with their living spaces. Many of us can live without fashionable furniture, new appliances, or multiple bathrooms. But none of us wants to live without comfort, and comfort often depends upon SPACE.

Ahh, space. Adequate space, generous space, liberating space—this is exactly what most of us lack, and, if current trends continue, coming decades will see more people living in less space in urban areas the world over. This should not be cause for despair. What this book intends to do is to demonstrate that limitations imposed by lack of space can largely be overcome by intelligent design, and that compactness in the home can in fact become a virtue. Indeed, this book would like to suggest that compactness, comfort, and convenience go hand-in-hand.

Some of the ideas presented here may seem extreme at first glance, but all were selected with current western lifestyles in mind. Many will be immediately attractive to those living in studio or one-bedroom apartments; others will appeal to families whose members are growing faster than their living quarters. Most can be adapted to existing space—retrofits, so to speak—while a few may inspire those people planning new homes. All have as their goal increased comfort—mental and physical—and greater pleasure in the home.

"What's the trick?" you may ask. Well, most of the ideas presented in this book come from Japan. Japan, whose urban areas are among the densest in the world, has a long tradition of dealing with limited space, so much so that it can be said to be second nature for architects, designers, and homeowners alike. The so-called rabbit hutches are fast becoming a thing of the past. The intelligence, cleverness, and refinement with which the well-designed contemporary Japanese home utilizes space can be astonishing, and the pace of development of new ideas and techniques can best be described as feverish. And, fortunately for us, most can be put to good use in the western home as well.

The fact is, the contemporary Japanese home has become very "western," so most of the ideas shown here won't seem particularly "Japanese." Although many of the more intelligent aspects of new Japanese homes derive from older Asian traditions, most Japanese of today switch easily from one mode of life to the other—from sitting at the dinner table for a meal to, say, sitting on the floor to watch television; from knife and fork to chopsticks. At the same time western life absorbs more and more "Oriental" influence—from cushions on the floor for lounging to compact stereo components and teacups without handles. This makes the adaptation of ideas easier in either direction.

Fig 1. Horizontality and the role of the floor: **a)** large area of shadow under table and chairs, **b)** less shadow under low table, **c)** figure seated on floor can be given privacy by waist-height screen which doesn't block much light.

1. This house in Narashino, near Tokyo, might be called a "modern traditional" Japanese home. While maintaining a number of older characteristics—such as the white rice-paper sliding screens (shoji), low table over a sunken floor area (kotatsu), and overall treatment of materials and details, it still has the freshness and convenience associated with modern comfort. Note the quality of the light, the clerestory windows which afford a glimpse of the ceiling extending outside, and the dominant horizontal lines, all of which make the room feel wider and more open even though fully enclosed. The tabletop can be set flush to the floor when not in use, and has a heating element underneath to warm the feet during winter months. (By Shoroku Tsukuda)

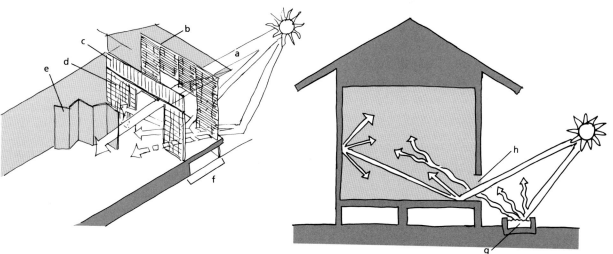

Figs 2a–b. Different types of indirect light: a) sunlight reflects off ground, b) hanging blinds (sudare), c) grille (ramma), d) paper screen (shoji), e) movable folding screen, opaque or translucent, f) many layers filter light, g) sunlight reflects off water, h) low opening admits only reflected light.

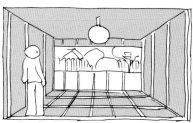
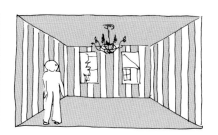

Figs 3a–c. Color and pattern
Fig 3a. Traditional Japanese room: light walls and floor with dark horizontal accents predominate.
Fig 3b. Light on dark, vertical lines feel claustrophobic.
Fig 3c. Very strong vertical pattern makes walls close in visually.

This book is not intended to give your home a "Japanese" style, attractive though that may be for some. It is about underlying concepts and concrete solutions to specific problems. And yet, many of the concepts are rooted in tradition. Apart from the fact that the Japanese have always taken small spaces, indeed all manner of small things, seriously, there has always been a tendency to value the compact and flexible over the massive and immovable. More specifically, there has always been an emphasis on lowness and horizontality, a dynamic interrelationship between living and storage zones, extensive use of modular, rearrangable cabinetry, and a particular attention to the nuances of lighting, color, and pattern. Perhaps these points should be explored in greater detail at the outset:

HORIZONTALITY: The greatest single advantage of retaining a low, horizontal orientation in living space is that *smaller spaces feel larger.* The psychological and perceptual mechanism by which this occurs is still poorly understood, but there seems to be a ratio between perceived horizontal expanse and perceived vertical limit—partly culturally dependent, of course—which determines whether one feels confined or unconstricted. Of course, a

lot depends upon the surrounding surfaces, their color and material, the prevailing light, and other elements which attract one's attention. But basically, when one is seated on the floor, the ceiling is farther away than it would be if one were seated on a chair or standing, and the field of vision naturally adjusts itself to be more sensitive of features which lie within the horizontal "sandwich" of space defined by one's body. Small horizontal changes of level have greater impact, and less is required to bound the space. Of course, to live low to the floor one needs to have less on it, and that smaller and easily movable; this enhances the feeling of emptiness, and can mentally magnify even a small room.

LIGHTING AND COLOR/PATTERN: Primarily, direct light is avoided in favor of indirect, filtered, or reflected light. The main practical reason for this is that a shady interior is cooler than one which receives sun directly. Beyond this, filters—such as translucent screens, wooden grilles, and hanging blinds—help create the illusion of great spatial depth, especially when used cleverly in an overlapping manner. Similarly, allowing the interior to be partially illuminated by reflections from a light-colored ground or water surface outdoors can provide a pleasant illusion of an insubstantial ceiling and upper wall.

Color, too, can be used to enhance or shape the living space. Primarily, light colors are better than dark ones for walls, but the ceiling should be a few shades darker than the walls. This way, the walls themselves won't attract as much attention, particularly if they are an even, restful natural tone, while the ceiling will seem to recede. Both the color of the room, and the patterns created by their elements, can be tuned, so to speak, to lead the eye to points where the room opens up, and to enhance the illusion of size, depth, and openness. Vertical lines should be used with great care, primarily as dark accents on a light ground, and should never be allowed to overpower the horizontals.

TAKING SMALL SPACE SERIOUSLY: It must also be remembered that, partly due to necessity and partly due to religious and ethical ideals, the Japanese long ago developed what can be called "an aesthetic of the intimate." Another way to put this is to say that this culture takes small things seriously—and small spaces are no exception. In the best cases, it is as if the artist—be he a carver of

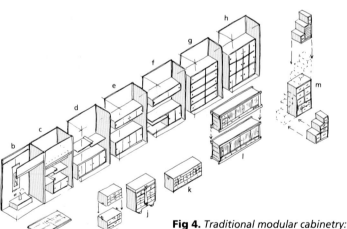

Fig 4. *Traditional modular cabinetry: a) tatami mat—basic module, approximately 3 by 6 feet, b) typical* tokonoma *decorative alcove with hanging scroll and display area for vase or object, c) staggered shelving (chigai-dana), d–h) variations on standardized shelving and built-in cabinets, i) two-piece stacking clothes chest (isho-dansu), many variations, j) wheeled chest (kuruma-dansu), made in variants for clothes, valuables, etc., k) clothes chest (isho-dansu), l) stacking kitchen cabinets (daidokoro todana), m) modular stairway chest (hako-kaidan).*

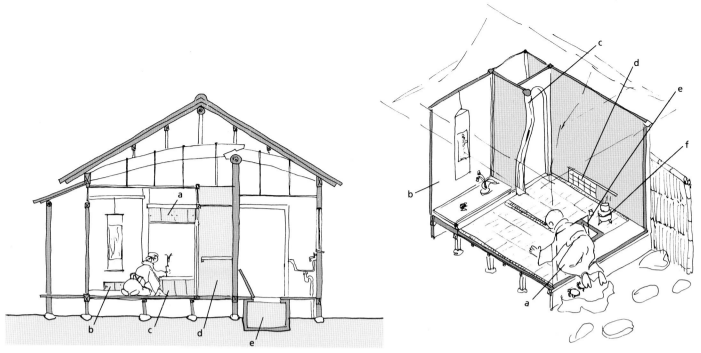

Fig 5. *Making use of the "unseen" space—storage zones in traditional Japanese homes (shading indicates storage):* **a)** *built-in cabinet at top of alcove,* **b)** *built-in display stand with storage within,* **c)** *built-in cabinet in alcove, shelf above,* **d)** *main closets, floor to ceiling, full width of wall, closed by sliding panels,* **e)** *underfloor storage for kitchen items.*

Fig 6. *Teahouse (chashitsu, mat area 6 ft. sq.):* **a)** *low entrance,* **b)** *alcove,* **c)** *decorative alcove pillar,* **d)** *low window with sliding screen closure,* **e)** *hearth,* **f)** *brazier for heating water.*

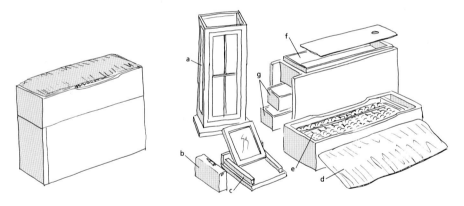

Fig 7. *Compact and flexible: traveler's pillow box—an early example of a compact, multipurpose device:* **a)** *floor lamp,* **b)** *sewing kit,* **c)** *mirror and stand,* **d)** *cushion,* **e)** *abacus,* **f, g)** *storage compartments.*

miniatures, a lacquerware craftsman, a potter, carpenter, or a painter of nature scenes—intends to entice the viewer into developing his own powers of observation. Entire worlds are suggested, in fact "conjured up" to be experienced, by the nuance of details. The natural world, of course, is both the starting and end point, and the traditional artist generally believed it could best be captured on a small scale.

This explains, in part, the impetus behind the creation of the first teahouses (*chashitsu*). Often no more than six feet square—and even less in one or two notable examples—the *chashitsu* was conceived as a place where one could focus one's attention on the intimate world. One of the paradoxes inherent in the teahouse—in fact, the

genius of the thing—is that when the setting and company are just right, one ceases to be aware of space at all. To speak of selfhood and existence here might be cumbersome and out of place, but in plain terms, sometimes all one needs to be truly content is a perfect corner, a good book, and a cup of tea. If one thinks about designing one's home as discovering what one's own "perfect corner" needs, then one will be well on the way to learning to appreciate a small space precisely *because of* its smallness.

COMPACT AND FLEXIBLE: Compactness and flexibility have been characteristic of the best Japanese design since ancient times. Poverty and lack of space may have provided the original impetus, but over time, designing and using these sorts of things

2. This generous house, called "Echo Chamber," demonstrates the power of suggestion and whimsy. Shoehorned onto a 2700-square-foot lot in a western suburb of Tokyo, the three-bedroom house still has room for an ample courtyard bounded by a wall which completely blocks out the street while "borrowing" the view of the trees beyond. An enticing shallow pool and play areas accommodate the needs of children, while large, fully retractable expanses of glass on the southern exposure allow passive solar heating in winter and natural cooling in summer (see also bath and kitchen chapters). By (Ushida-Findlay Partnership)

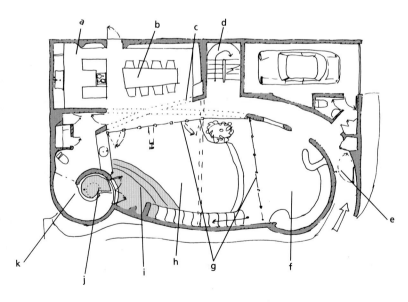

Fig 8. *Plan for the "Echo Chamber": a) kitchen, b) dining, c) beams above, d) stairs to bedrooms above, e) entrance, f) living, g) fully openable glass doors, h) courtyard, i) pool, j) tub, k) bathroom.*

seems to have become a primary source of pleasure in Japan—witness Transformer toys, collapsible motorcycles, and the combination phone/answering machine/fax/modem/alarm radios. Although Japanese today consume a lot and discard more, most still prefer items that embody the old virtues.

True, in many cases, optimum performance and durability is sacrificed for size and flexibility. This is the sort of necessary trade-off that all of us with limited space are faced with. But it should be remembered that in the home, the "performance" of an element should be gauged not by industrial standards or the whims of fashion but by how well it fits one's lifestyle. The goal is to reinforce your personality through customization, not camouflage it through conformity. Where this is the concern, any tool that works should be used.

PART I

Elimination, concealment, comfort: these characteristics are exemplified in the living space of this house by architect Shoei Yoh.

Perhaps now is a good time to stop and think about what space is. Space is subject to extremes of perceptual subjectivity. It is relative. It is unlimited but only measurable by boundaries. It is a potential. It is, oddly enough, everywhere else but here, where we are, in the volume displaced by our own bodies, whose spatial sensors goggle about balanced on the top of a precariously tensioned spine.

On the other hand, space is best understood by touch. It is literally inside our bodies, with which we constantly compare our surroundings and the potential goals and obstacles within it. It is understood in the gut before being measured by the brain. It is subject to illusion. It is imaginary.

Professional architects and designers are usually very good at measuring space and structuring it so that we rarely crash through flimsy floors or are crushed by falling walls. However, the perception of space—those things one notices when one pays attention to oneself paying attention to one's environment—is something anyone can develop. More than anything else, it requires a loosening up, a sort of soft-focus, which can only emerge when one stops focusing on disconnected details and sinks back into the viscous ambience of the world. It's something like the way one perceives things underwater—all sort of blurred together and motivated by the same palpable fluid.

The first section of this book will deal with perceptions. Having noted that traditional Japanese builders were masters of perception, of illusion, and of suggestion who bequeathed a yet poorly appreciated treasure trove of ideas, techniques, and tools to the present generations, it explores some of their more broadly applicable principles for the invisible multiplication of space. It won't teach you how to see and feel, but it should help give an idea of when and where spatial imagination and visualization will come in handy.

CHAPTER 1

THINKING MINIMALLY

Just how useful can nothing be? Probably, where living with limited space is concerned, nothingness, or the appearance of nothingness, is an unavoidable first principle. At the same time, it is an elusive ideal which can be approached in many ways. It is, more than anything else, a mindset which prefers emptiness to opulence, silence to cacophony, and elemental timelessness to trendy "with-it-ness." The goal? Preserving the sense that one has ample room in which to move about, that all extraneous obstacles that could be perceived even subconsciously as contributing to a sense of claustrophobia have been, in fact, eliminated.

Of course, to western eyes, the Japanese often seem to be masters of eliminating the unnecessary. There are, for instance, the well-known "capsule hotels," in which the customer beds down inside a compartment no wider than a single bed and just tall enough to sit upright in (see *Afterword*, fig. 8); these have spawned "capsule offices" as well as "capsule apartments," in the denser urban areas. The people who use them consider the payoff in price and convenience worth the austerity. Then there are designs, indeed a trend, towards the look and feel of "minimalism" for its own sake. In certain outstanding cases, such as architect Tadao Ando's Sumiyoshi House of 1975, the "bare bones" aesthetic has developed into an image of discipline, toughness, and indestructibility, all the while maintaining a very modernist sense of composition and lighting that borders on the spectacular. This sort of lean, streamlined building can certainly be developed into comfortable, pleasant living quarters, especially through sensitive use of wood, fabric, and other gentle materials. Meanwhile, the clarity and unclutteredness of the Sumiyoshi house points in a promising direction.

Other designers, such as Toyo Ito, have experimented with ultrasimple housing structures which seem, and in many cases are, temporary (fig. 2); living in such a house would not seem to require discipline as much as a strong sense of self-sufficiency, since the house becomes more like oversized luggage for storing absolute necessities than a permanent base

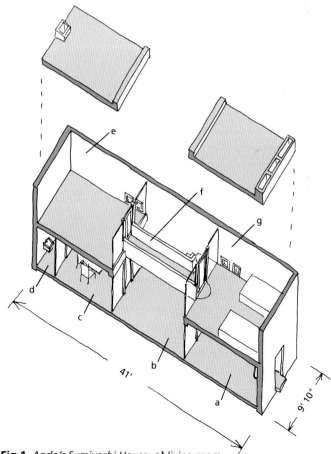

Fig 1. Ando's Sumiyoshi House: **a)** living room, **b)** courtyard, **c)** dining/kitchen, **d)** bath, **e)** spare room, **f)** bridge, **g)** bedroom.

4. Street façade.

5. Aesthetic austerity, by Tadao
Ando: View towards dining/kitchen
from open courtyard. Bridge links
second-floor rooms above.

crammed with things one "might need" someday.

The room by Shoei Yo (page 11) also says a lot. Although it could have been designed by any one of a number of skilled non-Japanese modernist architects, it shows evidence of knowledge of traditional Japanese architecture, particularly the way light is allowed in through little floor-level slits. In fact, like old Japanese houses, the entire wall is made to look like it can be easily rearranged. A table, a few chairs, a single light fixture—these can go a long way towards satisfying the essential needs of habitation. Everything else must be hidden away inside the floor-to-ceiling, wall-to-wall storage cabinets. The architecture of houses like this poses an important question: If you don't have space, how much can you live without?

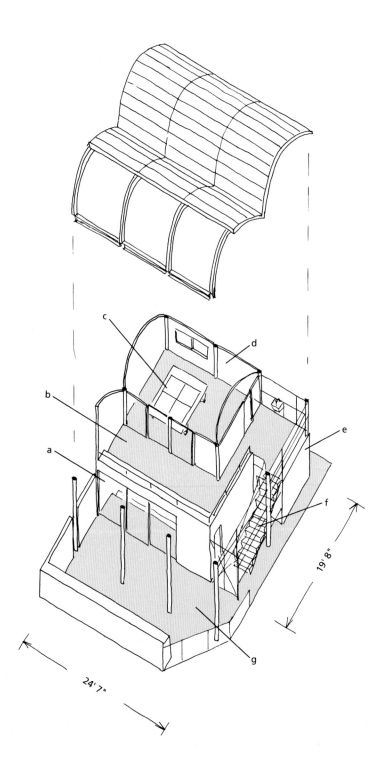

Fig 2. *Simplicity and richness, by Toyoo Ito:* ***a)*** *kitchen/dining/living in single space below,* ***b)*** *terrace,* ***c)*** *dais (raised platform),* ***d)*** *sleeping, private activities above,* ***e)*** *bath/toilet in wing (access from outdoors only),* ***f)*** *exterior stairs,* ***g)*** *courtyard.*

CHAPTER 2

LIVING LOW

nother basic principle of good Japanese design, both traditional and contemporary, is that of "living low." There is considerable speculation as to why the Japanese developed the habit of living on the floor; it is almost as if the entire house is one big piece of furniture, or one big bed. Today, most Japanese are equally comfortable seated on the floor or on chairs, although tables and chairs were popularized a little over a century ago. Nonetheless, the practice of living low has a lot to recommend it, particularly where one is faced with limited space.

Recent decades have seen an increase in experimentation with floor-level living in western cultures; low sofas, beanbag chairs, and futons have become quite popular within certain lifestyles. The primary advantage to low living is a perceived increase in the size of the room, particularly the ceiling height (see page 6, fig. 1). Also, the usual furnishings for a regular western room take up a lot of volume; they have legs or bases, backs, arms, and often approach the ceiling. More often than not, they block the light, creating a zone of shadow from waist level down. Good western-based design uses all of these characteristics to create dramatic, dynamic living space. But, if you don't

have the space to begin with, you might be better off concentrating on the floor: cover it with something soft, keep it clean and uncluttered, and provide inviting corners, elbow rests, and visual foci. You'll find that very subtle changes of level, color, or texture will take on an enhanced dynamism. Counters and storage elements can be kept lower, exposing more bare wall. This—also because the floor covering itself can be a more reflective, lighter color—means less lighting, artificial as well as natural, can have a greater effect. Above all, most people feel more relaxed and less formal stretched out on the floor or sitting cross-legged in a circle of friends. Assuming one suffers neither from excess dignity nor stiff legs, the spatial payoff can be quite large.

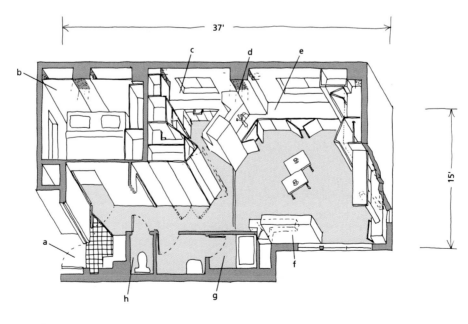

Fig 1. *Cutaway plan of one-bedroom apartment: a) entrance, b) bedroom, c) kitchen, d) beams removed for clarity, e) seating unit with storage below, f) TV, heater/AC housing, g) bath, h) toilet.*

6. This is the view of a renovated one-bedroom apartment towards the kitchen and entryway. Rather than separating the kitchen from the living area fully or leaving them entirely undivided, the designers have reached a comfortable compromise which admits light from the kitchen window into the living space, allows a place for the eye to wander outward and upward, and encourages conversation between the persons in the kitchen and those in the living room. The right-hand part of the diagonal partition, integrated with the low seating/storage unit, is only shoulder-height; behind it is a kitchen counter. The rectangular volume connected to it houses the refrigerator and additional storage; it works with the floor-to-ceiling cabinet opposite to create a kind of miniature architectural skyline. The interiors and doors of the cabinets themselves are particularly well thought out (figs. 2–4). Notice the slight change in floor level and material between the two zones. Also, the round protrusions on the ceiling beam above can be used to mount translucent hanging room dividers for a little extra drama, color, and/or privacy.

7. This view of the same room illustrates the most important principles of "living low." This room, 27 by 15 feet, is primarily used by the owners, a young couple, for living, dining, and entertaining. Futons for sleeping are stored in the floor-to-ceiling cabinet against the far wall, next to which is the primary visual focus of the room, a modernized version of the traditional tokonoma: a low shelf with a decorative column and space for a flower arrangement and/or artwork. In this case, the "artwork" is the colored design on the window glass; the lower shelf itself houses stereo equipment, and the cables for the speakers above are concealed in the column. To the right can be seen a built-in cabinet housing the television and the heating/AC unit, plus a low counter with drawers. The left-hand wall has a long storage cabinet that doubles as seating as well as a back/elbow rest. The room can be enlivened with a variety of throw cushions and low tables. (By Pittori Piccoli)

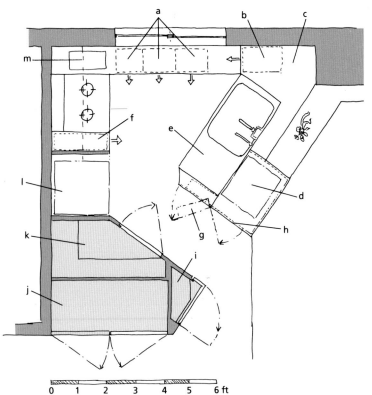

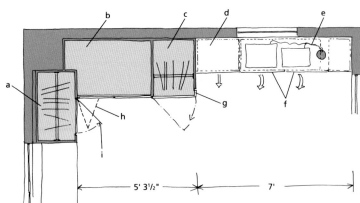

0 1 2 3 4 5 6 ft

Fig 2. *Plan of the compact kitchen: **a)** countertop with three shallow drawers, cabinets below, **b)** three drawers stacked vertically, **c)** eye-level counter, **d)** microwave enclosed at eye-level, **e)** waist-level counter, cabinets below, **f)** tall, skinny drawer slides out, **g)** door-mounted spice rack, **h)** access to storage under microwave, **i)** storage for cups, etc., with L-shaped door; shelf corners beveled for safety, **j)** linen cabinet, **k)** pantry, **l)** refrigerator, **m)** line of cabinets above.*

Fig 3. *Closet and stereo cabinet details: **a)** full-length hanging storage, **b)** bedding storage shelves, **c)** hanging storage, one rod above, one below, **d)** sliding drawers with cassette tapes, **e)** speaker cable runs up column to shelf above, **f)** front panels fold down for stereo access, **g)** L-shaped door, **h)** double-hinged folding door, **i)** simple door.*

5' 3½"   7'

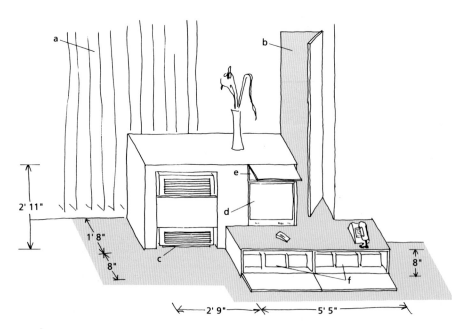

Fig 4. *Television and heater cabinet details: **a)** window behind, **b)** deep, narrow storage, **c)** heater/AC unit, **d)** TV, **e)** video deck, **f)** video storage.*

2' 11"   1' 8"   8"   8"   2' 9"   5' 5"

Chapter 3

A WORD ABOUT LAYOUT

Of all the factors that make up a successful small space, layout is the most important. Layout basically involves defining areas and connecting them. The type of thinking needed to lay out a space from scratch is different in some respects from that needed for conversion. Some prefer having a blank slate at the start, while others get better ideas from what already exists. Regardless, imagination is essential; though few realize it, the kind of imagination which allows one to see a completed room in one's mind's eye—visualization—is quite easy to develop.

It is possible, of course, to envision living in a single, undifferentiated space, with all storage concealed, for example, and all furniture on wheels to be rearranged frequently at will (page 12, fig. 1). In fact, one sometimes comes across successful living spaces made in this way. Still, even in such an extreme case, a few elements will probably be fixed. The location of the entry or entries, for instance, will probably not be variable; similarly, anything requiring plumbing, such as kitchen and hygienic fixtures, will probably have to be placed once and then not moved (though provision can be made for later expansion). If one assumes everything else to be more or less flexible, then in all likelihood an adaptable layout can be found (see fig. 2).

In general, one would like to separate living functions to give privacy and focus where needed, but not so solidly that the space ends up being chopped into hard cubicles. And, in many cases a single space will be allowed to do double duty—living and dining, sleeping and work, living and sleeping, or even everything altogether. Maybe the space will be divided most of the time and opened up for special occasions. Maybe the bed can be totally concealed and taken out only when it is to be used (fig. 4). Or maybe one absolutely needs an area set off just for work and nothing else. Most of these needs can be met through flexible layout, or what might be called the "soft" division of space, or again, through one of the most powerful tools, a change in level (to be dealt with in the following chapter).

One can begin by dividing space purely by means of ambient light—shadows for privacy, brightness for community, or even the other way around depending on your taste. Similarly, simple changes in color and texture can differentiate between and give character to different zones. A hard white tile floor in an area used for cooking might give way to grey carpet in the dining area, for

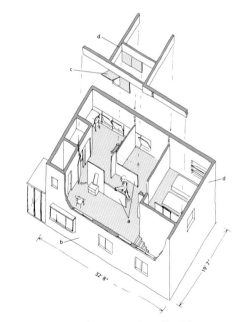

Fig 1. *Cutaway of house with its flexible partitions: a) fixed waist-high partitions, b) one-room living space below, c) hinged shutters, d) upper portion of wall.*

8, 9. Here is an excellent example of "soft" division achieved through a simple technique. The waist-high partitions gently delineate the space—less than 650 square feet—without fully enclosing it. The openings can, however, be closed when desired by means of hinged shutters (actually derived from ancient Japanese prototypes). Sliding doors complete the flexible, open layout, allowing privacy on demand. (By Jun Itami)

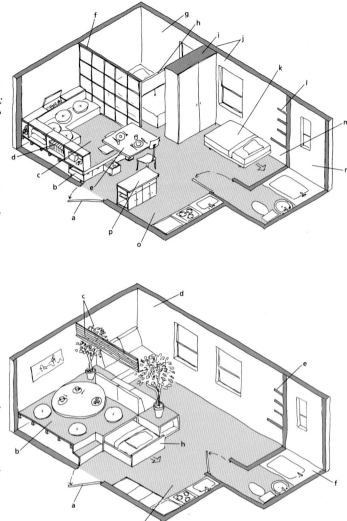

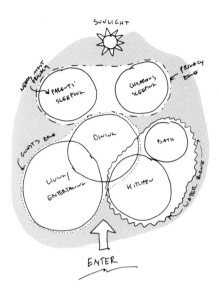

Fig 2. *Balloon diagrams like this can help determine how to divide your space. In the case of renovations, existing, unmovable features such as entrances and windows should be indicated first; when starting from scratch, a note about the direction of sunlight might be all that is needed. The room shown in figure 3 was generated from this diagram.*

Fig 3. *Sample room layout "A" using "soft division" techniques: a) entrance, b) pull-out storage units on casters, c) raised living area with low seating, d) storage behind seating, forms ledge for display, etc., e) fixed table for dining, etc. (chairs on one side, cushions on platform opposite), f) fixed translucent screen divides living and sleeping areas while allowing light from window to reach living area, g) sleeping area, h) pull-down shade instead of door, i) cabinet serves as space divider, j) windows, k) child's bed rolls under desk when not in use, l) line of shelves, m) desk above, n) bathroom, o) kitchen area, p) kitchen counter conveniently placed near entry.*

Fig 4. *Sample room layout "B" using "soft division" techniques: a) entrance, b) raised dining area with fixed table (space below can be adapted for storage—see Under the Floor), c) living/dining areas divided by grille above, plants and seat backs below, d) living area, e) line of shelves, f) bathroom, g) kitchen area, h) bed pulls out for use.*

instance, separating the spaces without dividing them. Similarly jute wall covering in the sleeping area might segue into pastel-colored plaster for an area where guests might be entertained. Public and private zones might be cued by floor surfaces of metal and wood.

Thinking more definitively, the use of partial partitions, extending from the floor to waist or chest height, can provide an ample sense of separation, especially while one is seated, without losing the sense of openness (plates 8, 9, fig. 1). These low partitions can be in the form of storage elements or furniture, and can be combined with matching or contrasting closures for the upper part. Alternatively, all can be movable and/or removable. We have even seen instances where a tent was set up in a loftlike area of an apart-

ment for coziness and privacy.

Learning to see opportunities to combine functions encourages a playful spirit, and is one of the best ways to allow one's individuality to emerge. Maybe the bed should go on top of the dresser, the pantry under the floor, the bathtub on the balcony. Maybe a single long table can comfortably accommodate three dinner guests, the coffee maker, and a word processor. Maybe there's only one window, and you'll want to find a way to place your worktable near it for daytime use, while also making room for the bed so you can wake up to sunlight. There's no need for a combinatory approach to lead to a makeshift feeling or to call attention to a space's inadequacies. On the contrary, points like these should be sought out as opportunities for personal expression.

CHAPTER 4

LEVEL CHANGE

One of the most useful and hence most frequently seen methods of separating interior space without the use of walls is to set it off by means of a change in floor level.

A level change of only a few inches, perhaps accompanied by a change in floor covering, can easily set off a space for relaxing, sitting, or talking from one used for standing, movement, or storage. A section of the floor can even be raised high enough to allow significant storage underneath (see *Under The Floor*). Similarly, a change in ceiling height can be effective in setting off a small area for a specific use; if the change is great enough, the space above can be freed for other uses, ranging from book storage to a sleeping loft. The floor and/or ceiling height change may be accompanied by vertical partitioning of some sort—curtains, shelving, or sliding panels, for instance, depending upon the circumstances (see *A Word About Layout*).

Of course, the effect of a change in level is amplified by an accompanying modification of light, material, color, or texture as discussed earlier. The addition of accenting elements such as shelves, moldings, niches, or even a picture on the wall can help integrate the raised level visually. The eye usually seeks out light sources and strives to recognize individual contrasting elements in the brief split second before it calculates floor heights, wall angles, ceilings, and so on (probably a holdover from the time when an in-

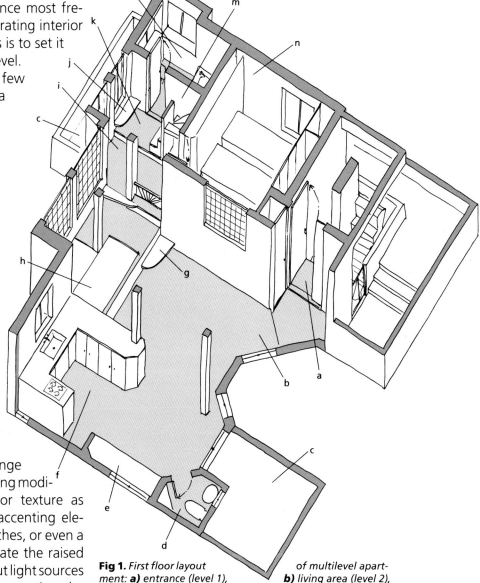

Fig 1. *First floor layout of multilevel apartment:* ***a)*** *entrance (level 1),* ***b)*** *living area (level 2),* ***c)*** *outdoor terraces (there are three),* ***d)*** *toilet/lavatory,* ***e)*** *built-in seating nook for dining,* ***f)*** *dining area (level 2),* ***g)*** *step,* ***h)*** *tatami-floored seating nook (level 3),* ***i)*** *bedroom landing (level 4),* ***j)*** *display shelf,* ***k)*** *stair landing (level 5),* ***l)*** *main bathroom (level 6),* ***m)*** *stairway,* ***n)*** *master bedroom.*

10, 11. This Tokyo apartment demonstrates the use of levels in a spectacular way. The 710-square-foot first floor is divided into six levels (fig. 1), plus a small display shelf at the farthermost corner. Stairs lead to a 228-square-foot loft above. The entrance is on the lowest level, with living, dining, and kitchen on the second (and largest) level. A tatami-floored seating nook is on the third. The fourth level leads to the master bedroom, and the fifth to the stairway. The bathroom occupies the sixth level. The master bedroom opens onto the living area by means of shoji screens. The floor surface changes from stone in the entry, to dark natural wood, to tatami, to cork flooring, to tile in the bathroom. The loft space on the second floor creates the lowered ceiling area on the first, and also opens onto it by means of low windows. Columns are well-placed to enhance the soft division of the space. All in all a brilliant and attractive design, sparked by the need to accommodate enclosed parking below the bedroom! (By Atelier Mobile)

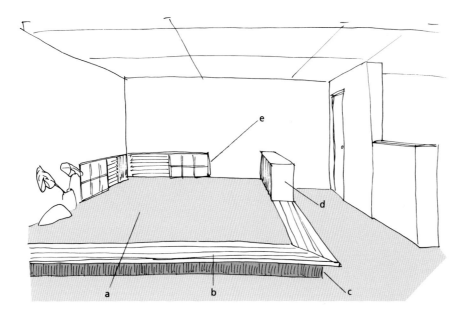

Fig 2. *A special nook made simply but effectively by means of a small change in level and low windows:* ***a)*** *carpeted floor,* ***b)*** *wood surface,* ***c)*** *eight-inch rise,* ***d)*** *cabinet,* ***e)*** *low windows with translucent shutters.*

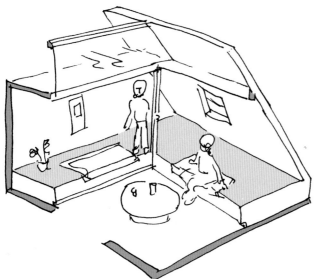

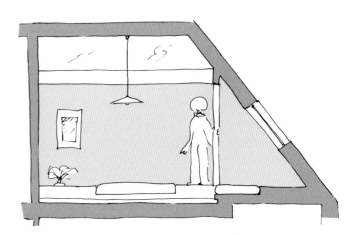

Figs. 3a–b. *Use of level change to form low seating, creating comfortable, well-lit nooks.*

stant instinctual understanding of unfamiliar surrounding was a matter of survival). So, making your levels seem more like the location of desirable goals—sunlight on a wooden sculpture, inviting pillows, a bowl of tropical fruit—will allow the actual level change to be perceived as prologue to the consummation, not as an intrusion. No one, after all, wants to stumble over a threshold for no reason.

Finally, levels may be required for practical reasons—to accommodate a garage below, to house the plumbing for a retrofit bathroom, or simply because the floor needs a new surface. In such cases, the need becomes an opportunity, but one which may require compromises. On the other hand, one may want levels just for fun. No problem there: just imagine yourself floating around the room, magic-carpet–style, and pick an attractive spot to settle several inches off the floor.

CHAPTER 5

BRINGING OUTSIDE IN

For making a room feel less confining and more spacious, probably no other design device is as effective as providing a visual connection to the outdoors, what we will call here "bringing outside in." While this can take a bewildering variety of forms, the only constant, essential feature to keep in mind is that while seated inside, one must have the sense that the (hopefully pleasant) outdoors are nearby and easily accessible.

For homes in constricted locations, this generally means providing a small garden that can be viewed from inside through a window of some sort. Alternately, the "view" can be of scenery in the near distance (see page 10, plate 2), or a small patch of sky. Even manmade scenery, such as an attractive nearby building, can be used as an aesthetic foil to draw one's attention outside. It is also possible to use a small piece of outdoor space in such a way as to suggest the presence of a view where none actually exists.

But of course, ideally, there should be greenery. Better still, the "garden" should be accessible, large enough to enter. At the same time, one should remember the power of suggestion: it isn't necessary to install floor-to-ceiling picture windows in order to "connect" inside with out. A small window, maybe shaded, even placed higher or lower than normal, is usually more effective in creating the illusion of an adjoining space so expansive that to show it all would be overpowering.

Some of the most effective "outside-in" designs involve actually letting the living space wrap around a small piece of outdoor space, giving the effect that the outside is actually penetrating the indoors (plates 12, 13). In Japan, this was often done through the use of a small garden called a *tsuboniwa*, or "half-mat" garden, sort of a shel-

tered, very small, nook of greenery the size of a small closet (fig. 3). Nowadays, a similar effect might be obtained through a small enclosed balcony with potted plants (fig. 6) and a glass door, or through a small light well of some sort (fig. 7). Similarly, the traditional *shoin* study nook, which usually featured a low desk in a corner set level

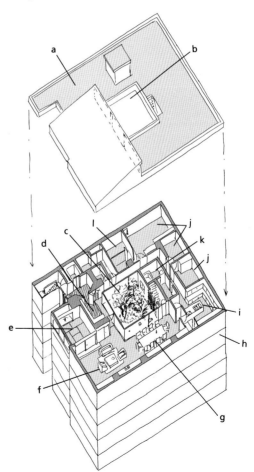

Fig 1. *Bird's-eye view of midtown apartment with central garden:* ***a)*** *roof,* ***b)*** *open to garden below,* ***c)*** *garden,* ***d)*** *entrance,* ***e)*** *Japanese-style room,* ***f)*** *living,* ***g)*** *dining,* ***h)*** *four floors of offices below,* ***i)*** *kitchen,* ***j)*** *bedrooms,* ***k)*** *bath,* ***l)*** *walk-in closet.*

12, 13. This strikingly verdant living space is on the fifth floor of a building tightly hemmed in on all sides by even taller office blocks in downtown Tokyo. While the floor space of this apartment is ample, its midtown environs create a feeling of cramped quarters, which is cleverly overcome by the garden at the center. If the garden were much larger, one would become aware of the surrounding sky-line; as it is, it is large enough to be entered, and has enough variety to reflect seasonal changes. While the detailing of this apartment is fairly modern in the international sense, the layout of the space, particularly the manner in which the main living areas and the corridor on the opposite side wrap around the garden, derives from Japanese residential tradition.

One departure from a tradition which prefers the best aesthetic experiences to be hidden—gardens like this would normally be located deep within the home and shown only to special guests—is that the outdoor space is the focal point of the entire home, and is visible from the moment one enters. The old, slow revelatory discovery is replaced by a thoroughly modern "bang-pow!!" (By Shimizu Corporation, Design Division)

Fig 2. *Floor plan and side views of apartment.*

Fig 3. *Miniature "half-mat" garden:* ***a)*** *garden,* ***b)*** *roofed verandas,* ***c)*** *sliding panels close off surrounding space.*

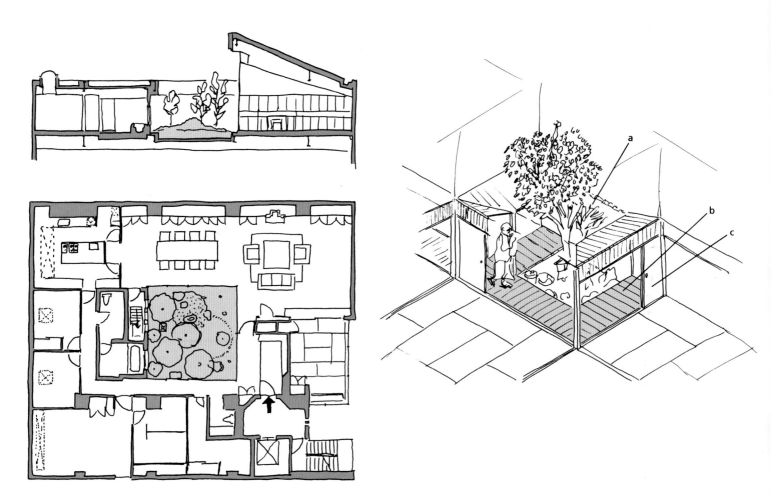

with a small window overlooking a garden whose light could be controlled through the use of translucent *shoji* sliding screens (*Afterword*, fig. 4b), has been transformed into a similarly scaled desk set in a bay window overlooking a small, green, enclosed terrace. The "garden," however it is conceived, needn't be big; it just has to feel close and have natural light.

Of course, nothing is wrong with providing an entire wall which can be opened and closed at will. All the better if the room can be thus "opened" at the corner. The problem with this in many situations is that it might let in a lot of unwanted scenery—telephone poles, garbage cans, the neighbors' bathroom window. But even less attractive views can be improved with clever framing and masking. Every gardener knows the trick of hiding the neighbors' driveway with high hedges; if anything, this sort of thing is easier in small spaces, where the garden itself is likely to be shallow and will probably be seen from only one position. The view, or field of vision, can be likened to a stage set; the key is to occupy it with what one wants to see, and hide what one doesn't, all the while remembering that a few items placed in overlapping layers, the tallest in back, with maybe one thin tall element placed to one side in front, can create a surprising illusion of depth and distance. Just give the eye somewhere to wander. Even a "garden" no more than two feet deep, set in the narrow space between houses, can be extremely effective in multiplying interior space.

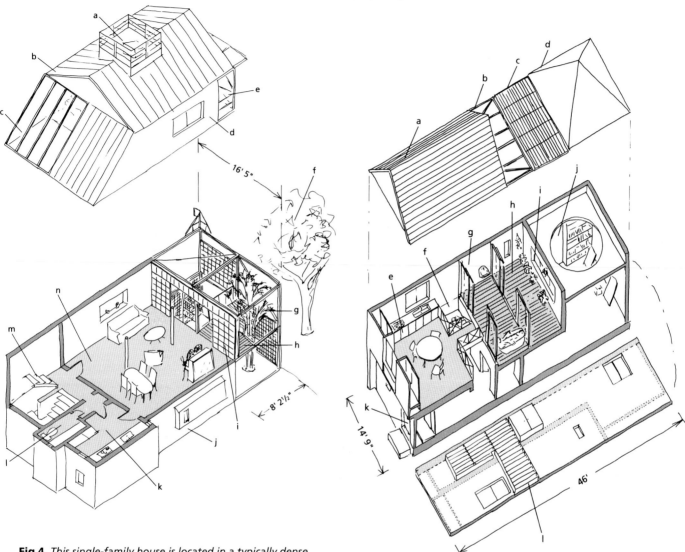

Fig 5. *Floor plan for townhouse (plates 14, 15) with "indoor courtyard": **a)** wood-frame roof, **b)** glass roof, **c)** trellis, **d)** concrete roof, **e)** kitchen/dining, **f)** stairway, **g)** glassed-in bath/laundry, **h)** courtyard/garden, **i)** window, **j)** open to sleeping/living space below, **k)** entrance, **l)** bookshelves.*

Fig 4. *This single-family house is located in a typically dense Tokyo residential neighborhood. The designer/occupant, Hisao Koyama, recognized that the narrow lot would allow flexibility and light only at the front and rear, and opted to create a patch of green at the front. Borrowing a few points from traditional Kyoto-type townhouses, and a few others from the English variety, Koyama placed the main living space on the second floor behind a screened, layered garden. A stand of bamboo is allowed to rise from the ground through an opening in the steel-grating balcony; additional green is "borrowed" from a large tree outside the property line. The entire front wall of the room is glass and can be closed off by sliding screens, which allow the shifting shadows of the leaves and structure to play upon their white background. components include: **a)** roof platform, **b)** roof, **c)** skylight over stairs, **d)** children's bedrooms, **e)** balconies, **f)** large tree, **g)** bamboo, **h)** balcony/deck, **i)** layered wall, **j)** bathroom, master bedroom, study on ground floor, **k)** kitchen, **l)** toilet/lavatory, **m)** stairway, **n)** living/dining.*

14, 15. This second-story space has a fine southern exposure and is given great depth and variety by being divided into three levels: the inside (kitchen), a glass-roofed intermediate zone (bath/laundry), and a terrace open to the sky (garden). Light enters both from above and through the gable-end windows, which lend extra drama to the rustic wood beams, here based on traditional farmhouse design. Although the house is flanked on either side by taller structures, enough privacy is maintained to place the bathtub halfway outdoors. Potted plants serve as a garden; a wire-mesh arbor has been provided for vines, which will eventually create a pleasant green ceiling for shade during the summer. Furthermore, this house is unusual in that the space wraps around the courtyard not in the typical horizontal fashion, but vertically (fig. 5). That is, the main living space is in front, below, and behind the garden, connected by a large window which allows a view of the first floor. In addition, the designer has mated a traditional wood-frame structure housing the kitchen on the second floor with a conventional concrete structure used for the rest of the house. (By Tsutomu Abe)

Fig 6. *A small greenhouse like this can take advantage of balcony or window space; raising it to waist height allows room for shelves or seating in front while making the gardening less of a back strain.*

Fig 7. *This small light well is more like a display case for nature; it could be made into a planted garden, or house a sculpture. Sliding doors at the back provide physical access, allow cross-ventilation, and connect separate living areas visually while maintaining privacy.*

CHAPTER 6

FURNITURE FOR SMALL SPACES

Nothing is more disastrous for a small space than dark, heavy wooden chairs and tables. Many seating and storage problems require ingenious solutions, but most needs can be filled simply. Modern, lightweight, visually unobtrusive furniture is not a Japanese invention, but designers in Japan have added incentive to put it to good use, enough so that one might rightly consider their use there a basic principle.

The fundamental idea is simple: assuming one has limited space and wants tables and chairs, these should be both as compact and as nearly invisible as possible. Furthermore, this kind of furniture works best with simple, light-colored floors and walls. Many of the best designs of this type date back to the twenties and thirties— Breuer, Gropius, Mies, Le Corbusier, and Eileen Gray are a few of the better-known early modern architects who also designed fine furniture. Some nineteenth-century designs are also quite simple, such as Thonet-style chairs, Shaker tables, and certain wrought-iron pieces. They, as well as the products of recent designers of all nationalities, can be quite appropriate. And there is no reason one shouldn't try to come up with one's own original solutions, especially with all the easily assembled modular systems currently on the market.

The "modern" style, of course, may not suit everyone. But still, if one basically follows the "doing without" principle, and keeps walls, floors, and other surfaces as uncluttered as possible, then one will be able to reap the benefits of added "visual space." In addition, assuming a small room and its furnishings aren't busy in appearance overall, one will probably be able to include one or two ornate or complicated elements, such as an elaborate framed mirror or an antique chest, without sacrificing the spacious feeling.

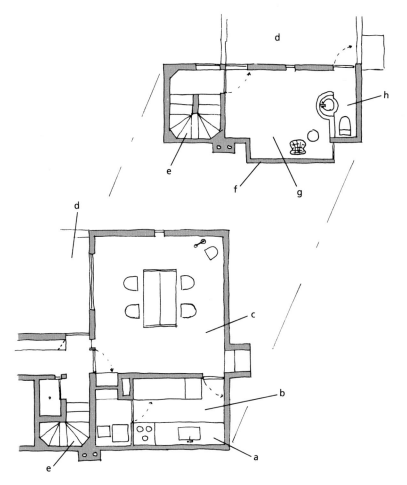

Figs 1a–b. *Floor plan for Hosaka House: **a)** main level, **b)** kitchen, **c)** living/dining, **d)** terrace, **e)** stairway, **f)** upper level, **g)** multipurpose room, **h)** toilet/lavatory.*

17. This is the main living space of an apartment built above a veterinary hospital which illustrates in almost textbook fashion the apparent increase in space that can be obtained through the use of visually lightweight furniture. Chairs, table, and lamp are all reduced to simple lines in space, and one can literally see right through them. The effect is enhanced by both the color and plain treatment of the walls and floor. Artwork, architectural details like the window recess, and color accents such as the door all take on a heightened presence. If anything, even though this room is only 18 by 18 feet, it feels empty. (Table by Mario Asnago and Claudio Vender, chairs by Regis Protiere, lamp by Cimini Tommaso; architect, Toda Ichiro)

16. Another room in the same house. A private space for reading, thinking, exercise, or maybe (with the addition of a futon) for guests, this room also carries restraint in furnishing to an extreme. The half-height partition hides a sink (in the semicircular niche, with a hinged circular mirror above) and, believe it or not, a toilet (behind the perforated screen). Table by Eileen Gray (1930s), chair by Harry Bertoia, (1950s), lamp by Y. Kaufman (1980s).

Figs 2a–h. *Classic lightweight modern furniture:* ***a)*** *"Cesca Armchair" by Marcel Breuer, 1928,* ***b)*** *"Vienna Chair" by Thonet, 1859,* ***c)*** *"Armchair No. 9" by Thonet, 1870,* ***d)*** *Dining chair by Robert Mallet-Stevens, c. 1920,* ***e)*** *"Viipuri Chair" by Aalvar Aalto, 1930,* ***f)*** *"The Classic Chair" by Hans Wegner, 1949,* ***g)*** *"Tugendhat Table" by Mies Van Der Rohe, 1930,* ***h)*** *Armchair by Josef Hoffman, 1890s.*

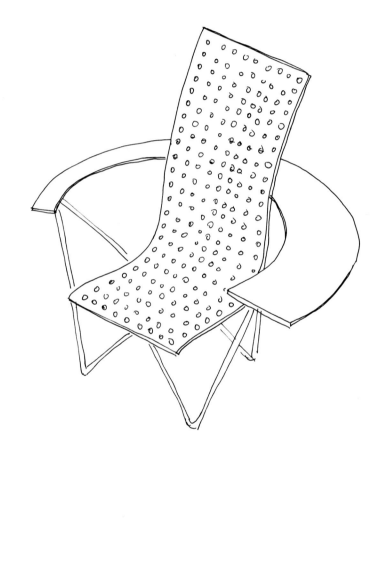

Fig 3. *Stackable chairs.*
This design solves the problem of space-stealing empty chairs in an unexpected manner: chairs are designed to stack, legs fitting into legs, taking up the space of a single chair when not in use. The designer has produced variations, and the idea may inspire original designs as well.

Fig 4. *"Fu-min" Armchair: lightweight chair of perforated aluminum with built-in side table.*

18, 19. Architect Toyoo Ito has designed some pro-
vocative and forward-looking hybrid furnishings—
which he calls "pre-furniture"—with the
single-dwelling woman in mind. Combining functions—seating and listening, makeup and storage,
clothing and decoration—these items are lightweight, fully portable, and nearly invisible.
    —"Pre-furniture for Styling": a combina-
tion of a mirrored dressing table and a wardrobe
(the large circular rack).
    —"Pre-furniture for Snacks": combina-
tion of tea table, shelf containing minimal dishes,
and cooking implements.
    —"Pre-furniture for Intelligence" (right):
a combination of a chair and a desk, with telephone,
walkman, clips to hold magazines, and so on.

PART II

USING LIMITED SPACE WISELY

As mentioned previously, so much of living small but comfortably depends upon spotting opportunities when organizing space. Another way to put it is that one should organize one's space in such a way that space-saving opportunities present themselves. For instance, raising sections of the floor not only divides the living space, it can also provide a few cubic feet of storage. Similarly, if one decides to include a solid dividing wall, it should probably be made thick enough to become a storage area as well. Accommodating one's needs in slightly extraordinary ways may sometimes add to construction cost, but as long as one doesn't attempt the ridiculous, room can probably be found for everything without breaking the bank.

People develop symbiotically with their living spaces. A person without a kitchen will probably never become a good cook. Needless to say, one should pay attention to one's current way of living to get a clear picture of one's patterns and habits, and try to create a living space which helps you to be the person you are. Like a jacket with an unusual zipper or a complicated buckle, sometimes items which require us to develop little routines actually enhance our sense of self; what at first seems simply awkward can become a pleasant, familiar ritual. There are limits, however. The idea is to avoid the stress that comes with inconvenience. Where do you like to put your keys? Near the door, next to the bed, or in the kitchen? What about the television? Do you like to watch it with friends in the living area, by yourself in bed, or both? Maybe there's a way to place it so both needs can be satisfied, and so that it can also be shut out of sight when your anti-TV aunt comes over. Having books or hobbies close at hand and visible can serve as a reminder to use them; party supplies or tax information can be stored more deeply, but not so inconveniently that retrieving them will seem like so much of a hassle that they will never be used. The idea is not simply to cram things into every available corner—although noticing available corners is the first step. It is rather to make a space which fits you like a pair of well-worn tennis shoes, even as you develop new habits.

Of course, storage is one of the greatest problems; one needs to find homes for a wide variety of items in different sizes, shapes, and degrees of delicacy and frequency of use. The other common "great" problem is having enough seating to accommodate guests when they come over without having a small room cluttered with unused chairs the rest of the time. Finally, there is the need to maintain the right flair or sparkle in one's home. No one wants to feel like they're living in—or visiting—a storage area. There should be room for humor, elegance, and poesy as well as your Frank Zappa records.

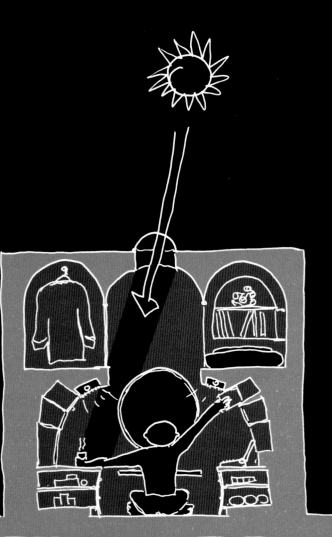

CHAPTER 7

UNDER THE FLOOR

Subfloor storage is a great idea. In various manifestations it has been used in Japan for a long time, but it is in fact better suited to western construction methods. By far the most appealing application is in the kitchen, where raising a small lid underfoot can reveal a few cubic feet of storage for canned goods, paper products, and the like (fig. 3); the lid can be made to match the flooring, not exactly hidden but nonetheless unobtrusive. In Japan, this type of storage takes advantage of the fact that houses are traditionally built raised a foot or so off the ground; the storage boxes can be simply cast in concrete and water-proofed (page 9, fig. 5). In other parts of the world with similar traditions—the southern United States, for instance—the adaptation will be very easy, and in some respects even easier in houses with cellars. Retrofits into concrete apartment blocks will re-quire more imagination, of course.

Subfloor storage boxes can be made to extend several feet under the floor horizontally, becoming more like a crawl space (fig. 5), even being large enough to hold several people stand-ing upright (and doubling as an emergency shelter, perhaps). Prefabricated units of this type are on the market in Japan, fully sealable, watertight, and shockproof but indistinguishable from the outside from the smaller version (fig. 6). We have also seen units with several cabinets which slide on or are suspended from rails so any one can be accessed through the small opening while the others are out of the way (fig. 4).

Raised floor areas can also be taken advan-tage of. Openable floor panels, covered with mats, carpeting, or other flooring, can conceal several square feet of usable storage, even if its only a few inches deep (plates 22, 23, fig. 2). Spring-loaded and hidden-latch hardware is available where se-curity is desirable. Where secrecy is less important than just plain storage, simpler lidlike arrange-ments may suffice. Variations include floors made of movable, modular boxes about a foot high, which can actually be removed for access and rearranged (fig. 7).

If one considers the floor to be the upper face of an otherwise unused volume, many possi-bilities will suggest themselves. Sometimes, for instance, stair landings could be potential storage sites, as could the space under bed platforms or

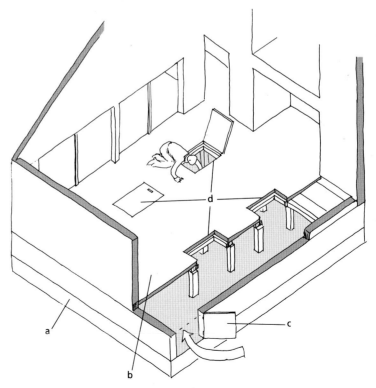

Fig 1. *Cutaway plan: **a)** concrete slab foundation, **b)** floor raised on struts (Japanese construction), **c)** street-side access door for storage of long items, **d)** access hatches.*

21. This is a studio in the home of an artist. This part of the house is built on short posts which raise it about a foot above a solid concrete slab. The entire underfloor area is used for storage of paints, wood, tools, and other materials. The sturdy lids are of the type made primarily for kitchen storage, with recessed pulls, here providing access to the single large storage zone at several points. The look is both utilitarian and a bit mysterious. (By Takamitsu and Rie Azuma)

Fig 2. *Side view: **a)** wooden drawers (6 each), **b)** sliding doors, **c)** flooring, **d)** wooden box (fixed in this case, but can be made removable), **e)** square tatami mat, plywood backing (perfectly flush when closed, removable with aid of upholstery hook). See photos opposite.*

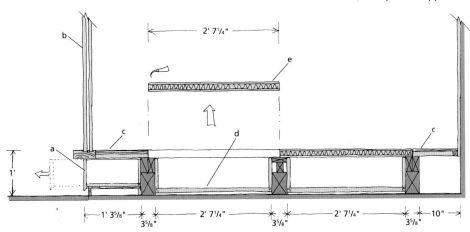

22, 23. These photos of a small house in Tokyo are almost self-explanatory. The small Japanese-style room is raised about a foot above the adjacent one, making room for two types of storage. The small drawers which fit under the decorative wood edging are used for frequently needed items. Still, when the drawers are closed, the unified white face does not call attention to itself. The spaces under the floor mats themselves are here lined with cedar, and used for seasonal storage of clothing. The mats themselves fit tightly, and a simple hooklike tool is used to pull them up (see fig. 2). The result is both secure and convenient enough for the infrequent access required. (By Shigeko Kato/Mizuki Kobo)

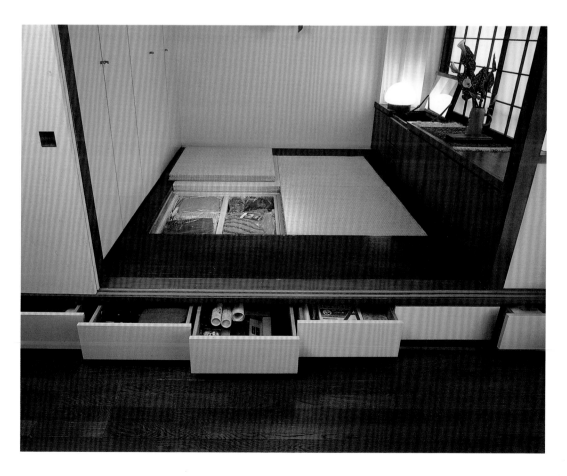

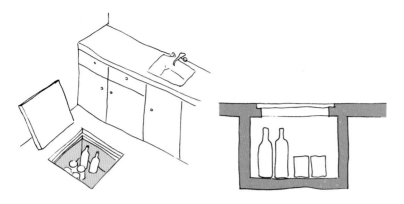

Figs 3a–b. *Simple subfloor storage box for kitchen.*

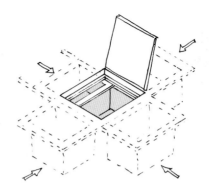

Fig 4. *Boxes slide on rails from four sides.*

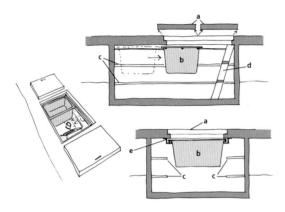

Figs 5a–c. *Crawl-space-type storage: **a)** two-piece lid, **b)** sliding storage box, **c)** shelves, **d)** access ladder, **e)** rails for rollers attached to box.*

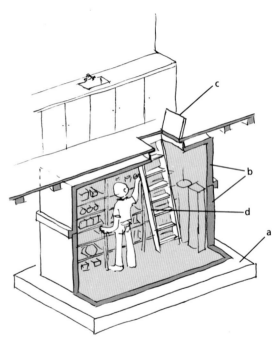

Fig 6. *Cellar-type storage: **a)** concrete footing, **b)** two-piece cast concrete structure (other material may be used), **c)** hatch, **d)** ladder (fixed is safer).*

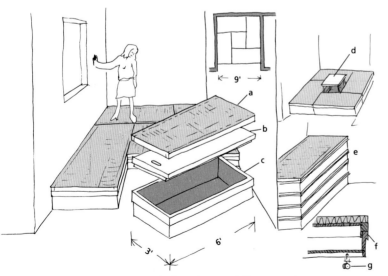

Figs 7a–e. *Modular, movable floor boxes: **a)** floor covering, **b)** wooden lid, **c)** wooden box, **d)** center box can be re-placed with table, **e)** boxes can be stacked out of the way, **f)** handhold, **g)** optional casters.*

lofts. One concept with enormous potential is the use of the front face of a raised area—be it floor, platform, or whatever—as an access aperture for the space behind. In many cases the structure will only allow storage a few feet deep there, enough for boxes of books, appliances, or toys, but on occasion entire beds can be made to pull out (see *Just for Children*). Ambitious plans like this will only be feasible if the layout of the living area is intelligently thought out. Remember, there is *always something* under the floor. If you think of it as a horizontal surface covering potentially usable space, what's underfoot might make your life easier.

CHAPTER 8

STAIRS

Stairs take up a lot of space. No matter where one puts them it seems that something else equally important should go there too. Most architects have not yet realized that it's entirely possible for two things to be in the same place at the same time, and where stairs for limited space are concerned, this approach holds the key.

One of the most brilliant traditional Japanese inventions was the so-called *hako kaidan*, or "box stair," essentially a stacked set of modular, movable cabinets which also served as an attractive staircase (page 8, fig. 4). From time to time similar items have appeared experimentally in western cultures—I'm thinking of mechanical library ladders which fold into tables or chairs when not in use—but the box stair is an idea with virtually no bugs. Furthermore, it can be used almost anywhere a regular stair can. By taking advantage of the graduated height of the stairs themselves this simple method can provide space for items of a variety of heights and widths, from comic books to skis. The next more elaborate manifestation requires the provision of drawers or cabinets which can slide in and out. These can also be made in a variety of sizes, either permanently connected to the stairs or entirely removable (figs. 5, 6). Drawers which emerge from the front face—the risers—of the stairs are seen more and more frequently in Japan now, as are treads which are hinged to open upwards (figs. 7, 8). Sometimes all these techniques are used to get the most out of a single staircase.

Also taking a cue from the movable aspect of the traditional box stair, stairs can be hinged or given casters, making them removable for extra space (fig. 9). Of course this may present safety problems in some situations, but particularly where the second floor is not in full-time use—like a sleeping or work loft—this approach has much to recommend it. The stairs can either be left in place most of the time and removed only for large gatherings, or can be stored semipermanently and deployed for infrequent use.

Stairs which wrap around a boxlike column or corner provide other opportunities. In cases like this, the stairs can be seen as giving access to a central "core" from different levels and sides. Similarly, railings can be thickened to give space for books or other items, either along the stairs themselves or at landings. The general unifying principle behind all these approaches is seeing the stairway as a volume which can be used freely as long as the climbing function is adequately and safely met. After all, most stairs are used for circulation several times a day at most, while whatever is stored in or around them will sit there almost all day long.

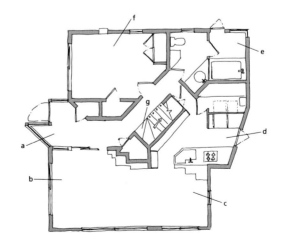

Fig 1. *Plan showing location of stairs with pullout storage in plates 24 and 25: **a)** entrance, **b)** living, **c)** dining, **d)** kitchen, **e)** bath, **f)** master bedroom, **g)** stairs. (See also* Disappearing Acts, *fig. 5, for layout of kitchen.)*

24, 25. These stairs are used primarily to reach the childrens' bedrooms on the second floor, and are near the bathroom and laundry. Taking advantage of this, the architect has provided fully removable rolling cabinets for storing underwear and towels, where they are easily accessible on the way to and from the bathroom. Also, the frequent stair climbing that would be necessary if these items had to be brought from the laundry to a storage place in the bedrooms upstairs is eliminated. (By Pittori Piccoli)

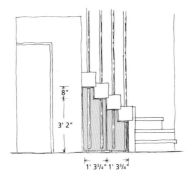

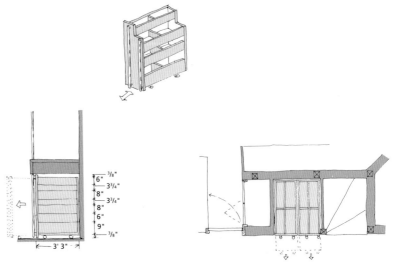

Figs 2a–d. Stairway details: section through storage wagon, typical storage wagon, plan showing location of wagons.

26, 27. This entrance hall shows just how elegant, practical, and unnoticeable under-stair storage can be. The entry serves several important functions. First, it makes a statement about the occupants which sets the tone for the rest of the home, preparing visitors for the atmosphere they are about to enter. Symbolically, the unusual ceramic fish here contributes to this atmosphere. Next, the single step provides a border separating the semipublic (and by association "dirty") exterior area where shoes are worn from the private (and hence "clean") home proper where shoes are forbidden. Lastly, and related to this, an easily accessible storage cabinet of some sort for shoes and slippers is provided, as well as a place for overcoats, umbrellas, and the like. Here, faced with a common situation in which a small lot means the living areas must be placed on the second floor, the architect has transformed the necessary stairs and landings into an aesthetic area with a strong but hidden practical value. (By Kenji Hongo)

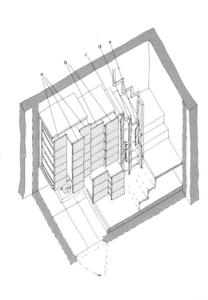

Fig 3. Entrance hall cabinets in open position: **a)** shoe storage, miscellaneous (upper only), **b)** shoe storage (upper and lower), **c)** overcoats, etc. (single door), **d)** umbrellas, etc. (single door), **e)** this cabinet divided into upper and lower, with two doors.

Fig 4. Entrance hall, details: **a)** niche, **b)** lighting, **c)** center cabinet (recessed over lighting), **d)** rear clearance primarily determined by narrow front clearance, **e)** cabinets open on one side for access, adjustable shelves, **f)** recessed for handhold, **g)** shoes, miscellaneous, **h)** shoes, **i)** coats, **j)** location of hanger bar, **k)** umbrellas, etc., **l)** miscellaneous.

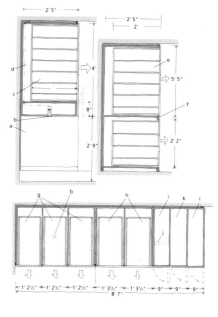

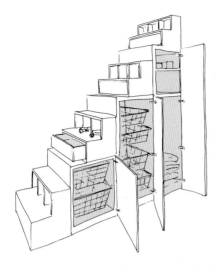

Fig 5. *Modern box stair with storage, version 1.*

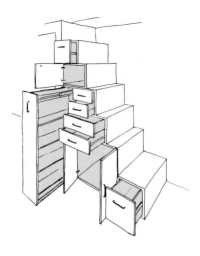

Fig 6. *Modern box stair with storage, version 2.*

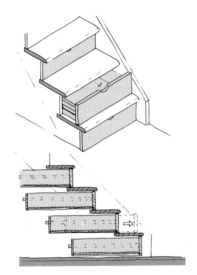

Figs 7a–b. *Drawers in riser face (note handhold).*

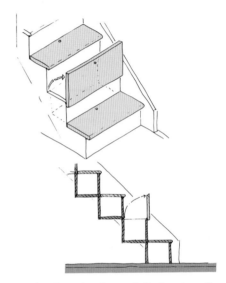

Figs 8a–b. *Hinged stair treads (hole acts as fingerhold).*

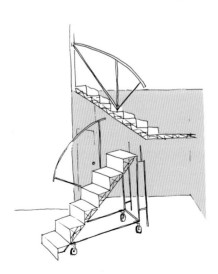

Fig 9. *Rolling staircase (can be moved out of the way when not needed).*

Fig 10. *Cabinets at base of stair only (provide usable storage while maintaining visual lightness of stair).*

CHAPTER 9

ODD CORNERS AND DEAD SPACE

deally there should be no such thing as "dead" space. One should be able to see all space as contributing something essential to life, either through utility—space to stand in, sit in, move through, set things on—or by providing a sense of freedom and expansiveness, as in space seen through a window. But the fact is, a lot of space in the average home is dead—killed by not being allowed to contribute to the occupants' mental and physical well-being. People can learn to ignore a lot of oppressions and inconveniences; but the fact is, if some part of your space is not helping your peace of mind, it's probably hurting it.

People in large homes can often afford to have a lot of "undetermined" or "underutilized" space. Those of us with space restrictions can't. Dead space is not the same as emptiness. Emptiness, or the illusion or suggestion of emptiness, should be considered a virtue. The idea is not to fill everything up, especially not if the result will be visual busyness and clutter. The idea is to notice the dead space and revive it.

In many cases dead space can be revived by small poetic gestures. There may be an awkward corner near your entryway which attracts your eye every time you go in or out, leaving you with an uncomfortable feeling that you cannot quite ignore. Your eye is led into the corner and stopped there for a moment, dead. Maybe that's a good place to put a shelf just big enough for a small flower vase and your keys, slightly below eye level (fig. 13). Maybe you have a tight staircase with a tall gray piece of wall behind it that always feels claustrophobic, causing you to want to pass by it as quickly as possible. That space could be revived by a tiny, slitlike window, for instance, that could also hold a single bud vase or a piece of colored glass.

Every home can benefit from revival in one or two spots. But, the principle to be remembered is that space should be revived by using the smallest gesture possible. Give your peripheral vision and your subconscious the benefit of the doubt; they'll notice the improvements, and you'll feel better.

There are perhaps a greater number of situations which call for more utilitarian revival techniques. Again, a look around will probably reveal a lot of surfaces which serve only to frame or outline other design elements—moldings around windows and doors, fixtures, the drop ceiling in

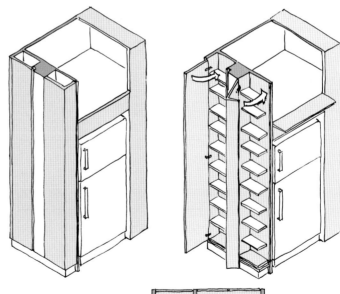

Figs 1a–c. *Kitchen wall storage: In figure 1b, the panel above refrigerator closes upward to hide large storage space above. In figure 1c, note the recesses at the edge of each swinging unit for handholds.*

28, 29. A wonderful example of "expanding" architectural features to accommodate extra storage. Typically, this thin segment of kitchen wall next to the refrigerator would simply be made of drywall. The architect, however, seized the opportunity to make convenient, unobtrusive shelving for tea, spices, and other small items (see also fig. 1). (By Pittori Piccoli)

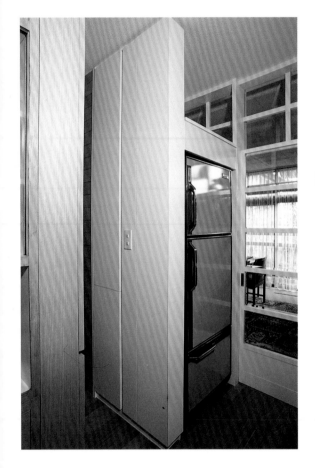

31. Often, when space doesn't allow the installation of a dishwasher, some provision can still be made for a dishwasher to speed the process. Here the architect takes advantage of what would usually be inaccessible inside corner cabinet space to install such a unit next to a gas range. Basically of conventional plywood and formica construction, the drying cabinet is lined in stainless steel and features off-the-shelf heating and exhaust elements. (See also fig. 3.) (By Pittori Piccoli)

30. The same designer found a way to "expand" the woodwork around this gas range unit to incorporate three types of shelving: a narrow drawer that pulls out from the rear, a set of enclosed shelves concealed by an L-shaped door, and open shelves on the opposite side. Take adequate fire precautions!! (See also fig. 2.) (By Pittori Piccoli)

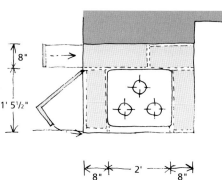

Fig 2. *Storage around range with regular open shelves on far side. (Again,* take adequate fireproofing precautions!)

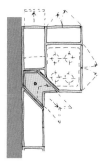

Fig 3. *Corner dishwasher.*

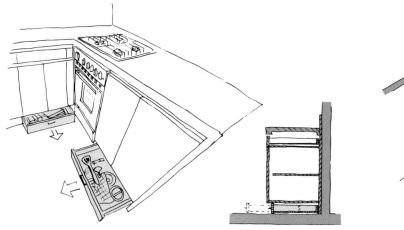

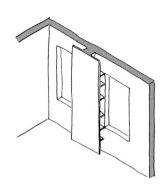

Figs 4a–b. *Reviving kickplates (drawer should be recessed a few inches when closed).*

Figs 5a–b. *Here a typical structural pilaster is widened slightly to accommodate unobtrusive shelves.*

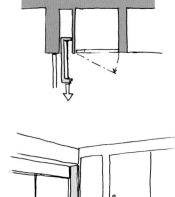

Figs 5, 6. Vertical elements. The various vertical bulges and moldings around the room also deserve attention. These can easily be modified to make space for tall, thin items, or items which can be hung, such as belts, neckties, extension cords, extra fluorescent light tubes. Usually all that's needed are a few inches, so these architectural features can be "expanded" without affecting the overall feeling of the room in any noticeable way.

Figs 6a–c. *A narrow, awkward piece of wall next to a closet is transformed into easy-to-use slide-out storage for neckties and belts which is nearly invisible when closed.*

the hallway. Assuming that one could still use more storage space, one might devote one's attention to these shadowy elements. Kickplates are a good place to start (fig. 4). One usually has them around the bases of cabinets in the kitchen and bath areas, at the bases of wardrobes, china closets, and other places where a cabinet is raised off the floor so that the doors may be easily opened. One can install drawers just a few inches high here that will be just right for bathroom scales, soap, or place mats. These drawers can be equipped with spring-loaded catches that allow them to be opened with a slight nudge of the foot. They will then be almost unnoticeable.

Some of the ideas described in this section will seem extreme to the point of desperation. But assuming one is going to spend the time and money to make a small space comfortable, one should remember that most clutter is in the form of small, oddly shaped items, and if one can find a way to make these things disappear into the woodwork, leaving the rest of the room empty, all the better.

Figs 7, 8. Similarly, it is possible to revive the dead space inside doors by thickening them, making cabinets on the interior surfaces of the doors (as is done with refrigerators) accessible from either inside or outside, or both. This can be carried as far as three layers of doors, all usable for storage.

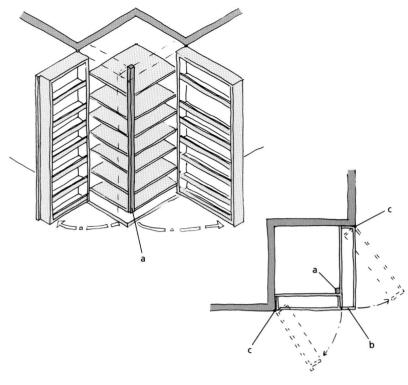

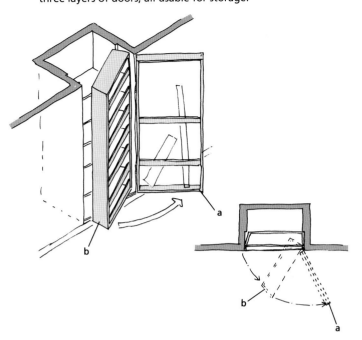

Figs 7a–b. *Double-doored closet: **a)** outermost door modified to hold tall, thin items, **b)** inner door fully fitted with shelves (note beveled corner for smooth closure).*

Figs 8a–b. *Corner closet: **a)** some structure probably necessary, **b)** note treatment of corner, **c)** hinge points.*

Fig 9. *Sofa niche storage.*
*Perhaps one's sofa area would actually be improved by being framed in a niche which would add usable cubic footage overhead and on the sides, while making the seat itself cozier. Components include: **a)** glass display cabinet, **b)** end table/shelf—for drinks, etc., **c)** cabinet.*

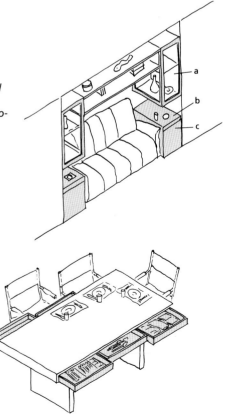

Figs 10, 11. The dead space inside furniture can be brought to life, for instance, by providing drawers for silverware within the thickness of a table top, room for magazines inside chair arms and backs, as well as for blankets inside beds.

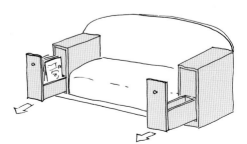

Fig 10. *Storage in arms of sofa.*

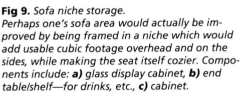

Fig 11. *Drawers for silverware and other table accessories built into table-top.*

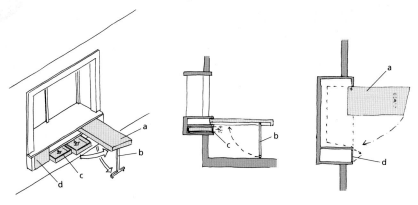

Fig 12a. *(Front, side, and top views) Desk/drawer combination:* **a)** *table swings out,* **b)** *leg folds down,* **c)** *drawers,* **d)** *cabinet.*

Figs 12a–d. Windowsills are another candidate for "revival." Tricks to be tried here range from shallow boxes with lids that fit the existing sill perfectly, to work surfaces which emerge from the space below or within the window. (Shown here is a prefab retrofit bay window unit incorporating drawers and a tabletop; these can also be custom-built, as can sills which incorporate everything from air conditioners to desks to bookshelves to sinks, none of which would take up any space within the room itself.)

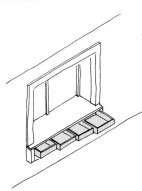

Fig 12b. *Drawers only.*

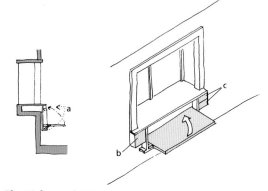

Fig 12c. *Sliding desk with central drawer:* **a)** *desk slides out,* **b)** *drawer emerges from desk,* **c)** *cabinet,* **d)** *room for drawers below.*

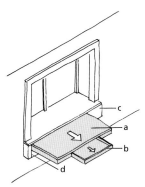

Fig 12d. *Low-height desk (for child):* **a)** *folds up, slides in,* **b)** *cabinet,* **c)** *drawers.*

Fig 13. *Reviving a dead corner: A simple triangular shelf makes sense out of an otherwise awkward corner.*

PART III

This 4' 3" diameter "kitchen island" has room for a sink, a double gas burner, three drawers, and ample below-counter storage, and can accommodate two seated persons comfortably. The only conceivable improvement would be if it were movable as well! (See also page 76.) (By Pittori Piccoli)

There are a number of other loosely defined but broadly applicable design strategies which can appear in different living contexts. For the most part, all involve ways of allowing single elements to fill more than one role, to take advantage of a "multipurpose" approach in order to simplify the atmosphere of the home. Some of the individual manifestations we have seen in Japan are quite remarkable in their intricacy; others merely required knowing where a fundamental idea could best be put to use. Yet any attempt to clearly categorize these ideas in order to explain them seems doomed, since they represent hybridized thinking. Nonetheless, the following sections attempt to illuminate some of the more important of these general strategies, particularly as they apply to specific areas of the home.

There are a number of ways in which giving elements of the home dual or multiple aspects can make life easier. One of the most often used techniques might be called the "disappearing act," which can be considered a specific kind of "convertibility." Most "disappearing acts" and "convertibles" involve movement, either in the form of opening, unfolding, or pulling out. In a number of instances, ways can be found to actually move an entire element—storage cabinets, for example—from one location to another. And, of course, there are a number of approaches which can be of assistance for specific applications, such as kitchens, bathrooms, childrens rooms, and the like. Again, the specific examples illustrated here might be tempting in and of themselves, but greater benefit can probably be derived by trying to grasp the underlying principles and then using them to generate original solutions to meet your specific needs.

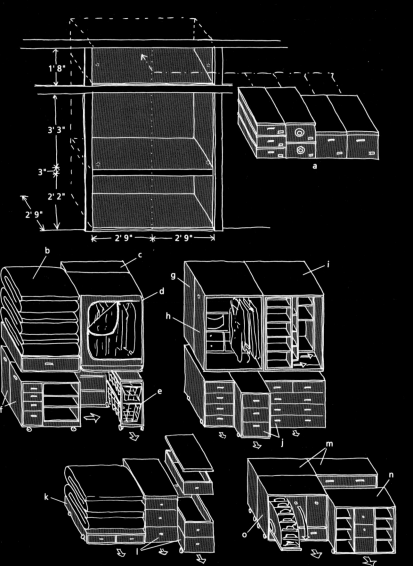

Figs 1a–e. *The modular closet.*
The closet has always been the ultimate multipurpose storage area of the home, but its true potential as such is rarely realized. Again taking a cue from Japan, where modular storage and commodious closets have a long history (see General Introduction), a number of variations on a standard theme are shown here. Figure 1a shows the standard Japanese-style closet, divided by a large shelf into upper and lower portions—both closed by the same sliding doors—as well as smaller, separately closed cabinet above. Dimensions vary slightly. Figures 1b and 1c show alternate arrangements for the entire closet, and figures 1d and 1e for the lower section. Components include: **a)** *stacking boxes for papers, seasonal items, and so on, go on top shelf,* **b)** *folded quilts (futon) on top of single low drawer unit,* **c)** *shelves for infrequently used items,* **d)** *zippered vinyl hanging storage,* **e)** *basket-type unit on casters,* **f)** *multipurpose storage units on casters,* **g)** *multipurpose storage for clothing items,* **h)** *open, box-type hanging storage,* **i)** *easy-access bookshelves (see Storage That Moves),* **j)** *drawer units on casters,* **k)** *folded quilts on top of low drawer unit with casters,* **l)** *stacked boxes on casters,* **m)** *drawer units on casters,* **n)** *multipurpose storage unit on casters,* **o)** *accordion-style shirt storage.*

CHAPTER 10

STORAGE THAT MOVES

Moving individual items into and out of storage is a familiar enough act for all of us, but storage which is itself movable can come in handy. It is also becoming increasingly common. The idea of movable (primarily but not exclusively *wheeled*) storage can be applied on many scales. Small wheeled boxes modularly designed to fit the standard closet space can make it easy to utilize the space way in the back (see page 60, fig. 1), while large bookcases which are partly on rollers can multiply shelf space (figs. 4–7). Movable storage can come in many degrees of formality as well, from rough cabinets, which can usually kept out of sight, to fine traditional or modern pieces which may act as showpieces.

There are many reasons why storage can or should be made movable, some aesthetic, most practical. It may be desirable to have the storage

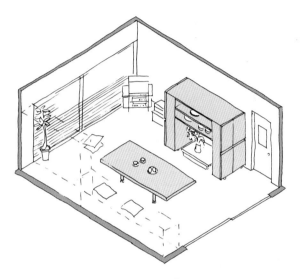

Fig 1. *Cabinet stowed against wall, table fixed at low height.*

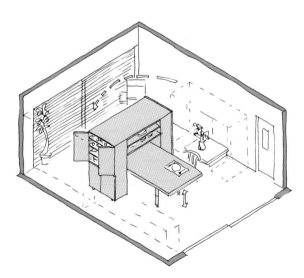

Fig 2. *Cabinet swung across room to act as divider, table raised with chairs.*

Fig 3. *Position for use as twin desks.*

33, 34. A small living and dining room is made more flexible by introducing two types of movement. First, the handsomely designed cabinet for glasses, crockery, and bar items can be rolled across the room to act as a partial divider, in which function it fits neatly over the table. Second, the table itself is adjustable in height—and also on casters—so that it can be used for both low and high seating (figs. 1, 2) or moved to operate as "twin desks" (fig. 3). (By Akira Yamada)

Figs 4–7. Easy-access bookcases.
This type of bookcase is quite common in Japan, and they are made in many variations. Basically, the front compartments are set on tracks for access to shelves in the rear. They can be two or three layers deep, and with compartments of varying depth and shelf sizes to fit the most common sizes of books.

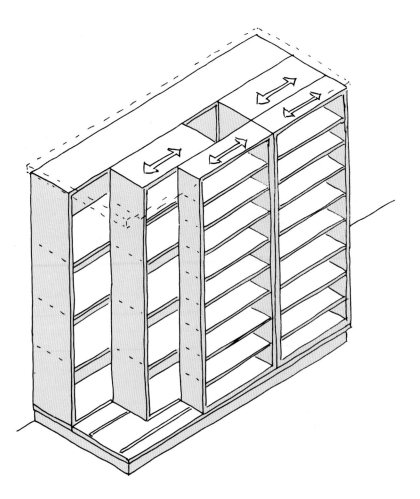

Fig 4. *Bookcase with three sets of shelves. Front compartments for paperbacks, mid-sized books in middle, largest in rear. (Top panel removed for clarity.)*

Fig 5. *Two-deep, stackable units.*

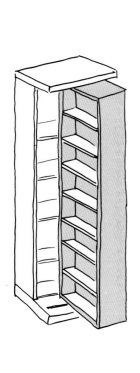

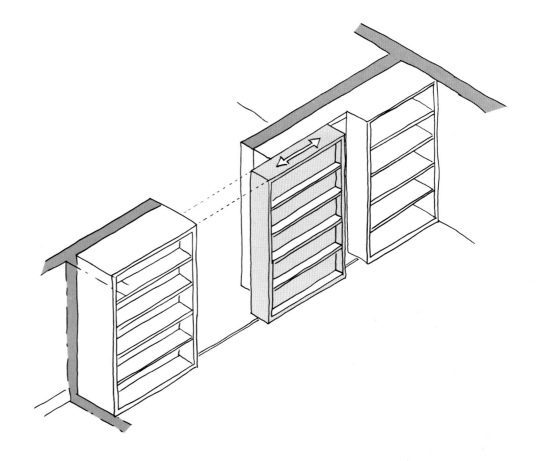

Figs 6a–b. *Pivoting type.*

Fig 7. *This is a built-in variant, where the movable bookcase also forms a sliding door between two rooms, with access to books from both sides.*

unit and the items within it disappear when not in use. Then again, what is inside may need to be used in more than one place. Providing movable or removable elements may make it easier to take advantage of "dead" space—unused space under the floors or stairs or in awkward corners. Sometimes, movable storage elements may provide a convenient way to rearrange the architecture of the home. The idea .of the storage cabinet as a room divider—bookcases, kitchens, counters, and so on—should be quite familiar to most; as such,

they can be designed for varying degrees of opacity, solidity, or openness, and can provide a convenient foil for color as well as sculptural statement (plates 33, 34). Of course, the most dramatic changes will be produced when the movable element is large, but smaller pieces, or groups of them, can also be very suggestive. There are few situations which cannot be improved by some sort of movable storage furniture. Getting the most out of it requires, as usual, thinking of ways to combine solutions to disparate needs in a single package.

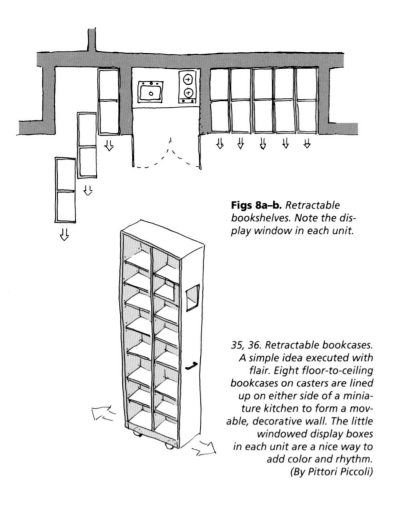

Figs 8a–b. *Retractable bookshelves. Note the display window in each unit.*

35, 36. Retractable bookcases. A simple idea executed with flair. Eight floor-to-ceiling bookcases on casters are lined up on either side of a miniature kitchen to form a movable, decorative wall. The little windowed display boxes in each unit are a nice way to add color and rhythm. (By Pittori Piccoli)

37, 38. Pull-out closets. Over 530 cubic feet of usable closet space is provided by mounting the closets themselves on casters. Various arrangements of hanger rods and overhead shelves enhance the overall flexibility, while the closets remain accessible from both sides and can be managed by a single person. When closed, the wall is flush and uncluttered. The dressing table continues the "disappearing act" theme (fig. 9). (By Pittori Piccoli)

39. Kitchen wagons. A great set of interchangeable rolling storage wagons for kitchen items which fit neatly under the counter when not in use, these suggest endless variations (see fig. 10). The pull handles form a line of trim when the wagons are stowed. (By Pittori Piccoli)

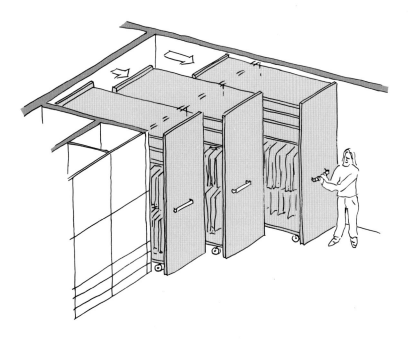

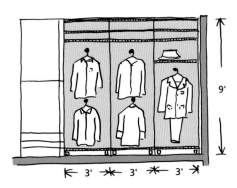

Figs 9a–b. *Pull-out closet. Open sides of three units allow air circulation and easy access.*

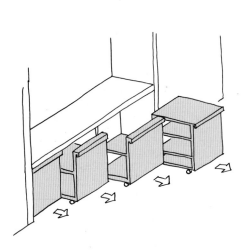

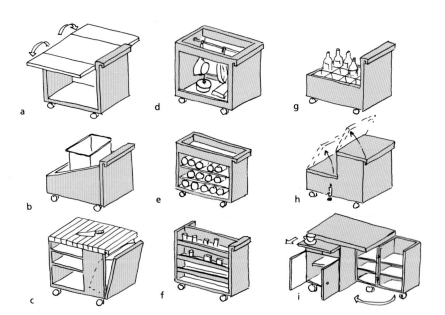

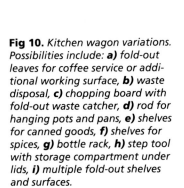

Fig 10. *Kitchen wagon variations. Possibilities include:* ***a)*** *fold-out leaves for coffee service or additional working surface,* ***b)*** *waste disposal,* ***c)*** *chopping board with fold-out waste catcher,* ***d)*** *rod for hanging pots and pans,* ***e)*** *shelves for canned goods,* ***f)*** *shelves for spices,* ***g)*** *bottle rack,* ***h)*** *step tool with storage compartment under lids,* ***i)*** *multiple fold-out shelves and surfaces.*

CHAPTER 11

DISAPPEARING ACTS

A "disappearing act" involves suggesting that what is visible—hopefully clean, uncluttered walls and surfaces—is all that is present, even when it isn't true. It's hard to say why a "disappearing act" should be different from something in the "convertible" or "multipurpose" categories (both dealt with in the following chapter). However, making things disappear when they're not in use is an idea at least as old as the first storage chests and closets. As for furniture, fold-down ironing boards, Murphy beds, rolltop desks, and built-in fold-down secretaries have been around in parts of the world for decades, in some cases, centuries. In Japan today, one can find a wide variety of similar devices.

Basically, a disappearing act has one "active" or deployed configuration and one "passive" or stowed one. The trick is to make both aspects fully satisfactory. Often function is sacrificed in order to make something easy to put away, while the look of the thing when stowed leaves something to be desired as well. On the one hand, it's possible to just hide things, or shut them up in closets, and even in such basic situations a little ingenuity can pay off handsomely. Or one can make the hiding place itself attractive, for instance, by integrating its visible face into the overall design. Sometimes it may be desirable to make the hiding place truly unnoticeable, whether to avoid cluttering up a wall surface or merely to keep a secret.

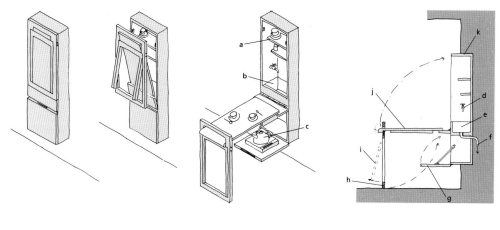

Figs 1a–d. Second kitchen.
This design provides extra kitchen space for making coffee, or preparing other simple refreshments, and eating breakfast. It houses a sink, hot plate, dishes, and so on. When closed, the simple face (each strip painted a different color) looks like pure decoration; the volume is partly recessed into the wall. The unit includes: **a)** shelves for dishes, etc., **b)** sink, **c)** hot plate is stored in lower compartment, whose door acts as shelf, **d)** faucet, **e)** stainless sink, **f)** drain, **g)** door folds down for shelf; note recess for grip, **h)** leg hinges backward, fits flush into back of tabletop, **i)** this piece hinged to accommodate notch in tabletop, lock leg in place, **j)** tabletop when open, closes into flush vertical panel, **k)** recessed space.

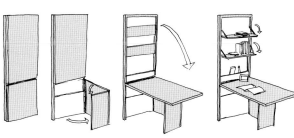

Figs 2a–d. Folding desk. This portable desk provides ample work space yet folds into a thin panel. Simple formica-covered plywood construction.

41. This dining table is designed to retract through the opening in the wall when extra space is needed in the living area—for parties, for example. The opening, which connects the living/dining area with the kitchen, can be closed by means of the simple shade above. (By Pittori Piccoli)

40. Folding lavatory.
Like the extra kitchen space (fig. 3), this unit serves as an extra bathroom sink. When closed, it looks like a colorful decorative panel, but opens to reveal a faucet, sink, toiletries, and so on. (By Pittori Piccoli)

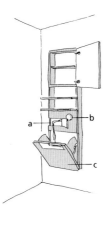
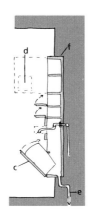

Figs 3a–b. *Components include:* **a)** *panel opens, faucet swings out,* **b)** *faucet knob,* **c)** *stainless-steel–lined sink front folds down,* **d)** *mirror,* **e)** *drain,* **f)** *unit recessed into wall.*

Fig 4.

42, 43. These two views of a small kitchen illustrate the advantages of simply having enough cupboards for everything, and of detailing their exteriors as simply as possible. Some areas which seem unlikely to be usable for storage—such as the corner next to the oven and the narrow horizontal strip at waist-height on the left—are actually usable space, while others which appear to be cabinets—such as the leftmost unit in the foreground—are not. Corners, hinges, and clearances are well thought out both for unobtrusiveness and practicality (see figs. 5a–b). (By Pittori Piccoli)

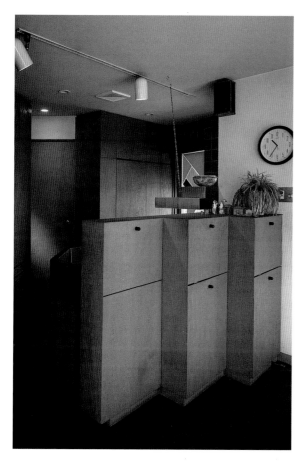

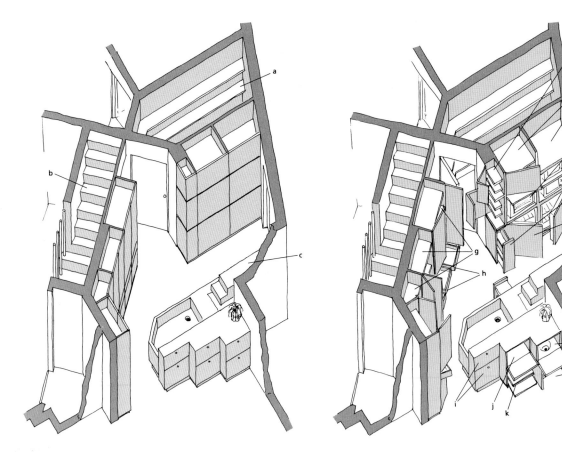

Figs 5a–b. *The "totally disappearing kitchen."*

Fig 5a. *Closed view:* **a)** *walk-in pantry,* **b)** *stairway (shown in plates 24, 25),* **c)** *range hood.*
Fig 5b. *Open view:* **a)** *corner cabinet for cups, condiments, etc; closed by upper and lower L-shaped doors,* **b)** *miscellaneous storage, simple hinged doors,* **c)** *oven; door pivots up, slides back out of the way,* **d)** *toaster oven and microwave, simple hinged door,* **e)** *slide-out spice rack,* **f)** *built-in refrigerator/freezer,* **g)** *all dishes, simple hinged doors,* **h)** *shallow drawers for silverware,* **i)** *dummy cabinets (sink behind),* **j)** *toaster (fold-down door),* **k)** *rice cooker, hot-water pot on slide-out shelves, simple door,* **l)** *water supply, sink for coffee (fold-down door),* **m)** *coffee supplies.*

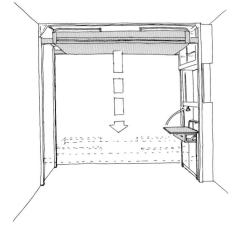

Fig 6. *Space bed. Now being mass-produced by a Japanese manufacturer, these beds retract to the ceiling. A number of styles and variations are available, including bunk beds; some are crank-operated, some electrically operated. A desktop/work space opens out when bed is raised.*

Alternately, leaving some suggestion of concealed potential, especially if curiosity is rewarded with surprise, can lead to very satisfying pleasures of another sort. And, don't be shy about including "fake" doors, panels, handles, or whatever. Sometimes they're called for by the need for symmetry, at other times no justification other than fun is required. But for the most part, psychological needs will best be filled by effectively suggesting emptiness, even when one knows it isn't true.

Finally, one should give some thought to exactly where whatever it is that's being hidden will disappear *to*. Walls are a prime candidate for many applications, and we've already seen how useful the floor can be. The same is true of the ceiling, though anything large or heavy will probably require professional engineering. Although the many factory-built "disappearing" or converting products—including beds which rise to the ceiling and televisions which pop out of kitchen counters—may not be easily available outside Japan, simpler, custom-made versions might prove feasible. One shouldn't assume that anything unusual will be prohibitively expensive; as always, apply a little imagination and answers will suggest themselves.

CHAPTER 12

CONVERTIBLE AND MULTIPURPOSE

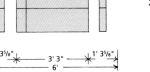

There may be a few items which serve more than one role, but are neither really movable nor disappearing, which we might nevertheless call "multipurpose." A good example of this would be the familiar American-style futon-sofa (fig. 3). (I say "American-style" because this is a peculiarly American idea which suits American sleeping and seating habits, but invariably strikes the Japanese as odd. Of course, like its ancestor, the convertible sofa, it saves space.)

Most multipurpose furnishings will probably be useful primarily because of their simplicity. Ideas like finding a wide-topped stool which can serve as a side table have occurred to nearly everyone at least once. Another example might be rigging a folding screen to separate a sleeping and dressing area from a living area, with full-length mirrors on the dressing side. This sort of item could be elaborated with hooks or pegs to accommodate clothing or accessories, and even some sort of lighting (fig. 4). Although part of its usefulness would come from its ability to be folded and stored away, it would be useful even if it were always left in place.

Tables present good opportunities for multipurpose treatment. Especially where one has room for only one table, and needs to use it for work as well as eating and entertaining, it may be a good idea to make or find one whose width and height can be changed. Tables like these have existed in western countries for centuries, but the ability of a single table to accommodate both floor- and chair-height seating allows much more dramatic changes in interior space. Of course, there's no reason such a table cannot also incorporate storage or even cooking facilities. The latter idea can be developed even further, with a single island like table housing everything from cooking sur-

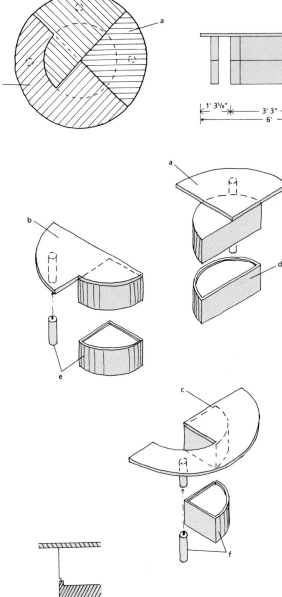

Figs 1a–d. *Multipurpose table.*

Fig 1a. *View showing how three tabletop sections fit together.*
Fig 1b. *Side view: The bottom section of the legs and base are removed for a low coffee table.*
Fig 1c. *Exploded view* UPPER LEVEL—TABLE HEIGHT: **Section a,** *quarter-circle top, half-cylinder base, leg;* **section b,** *modified half-circle top, quarter-cylinder base, leg;* **section c,** *modified half-circle top, quarter-cylinder base, leg;* LOWER LEVEL—FLOOR HEIGHT: **Section d,** *half-cylinder base, leg;* **section e,** *quarter-cylinder base, leg;* **section f,** *quarter-cylinder base, leg.*
Fig 1d. *Cross section showing how top and bottom sections fit together.*

44–50. *A simple idea well executed, or rather, an idea which is not really as simple as it looks. This modular table is composed of nine parts (including three leg extensions), which allows an almost endless variety of configurations, and also lends color and a playful spirit to the room. Here, of course, it is coupled with a semicircular seating niche, but the idea has wide applications. This unit can accommodate various seating heights and is even useful for work; although not done here, the hollow volumes could easily be adapted for storage (see figs. 1a–d). (By Pittori Piccoli)*

faces to a sink to storage for food, dishes, and silverware; it might even accommodate a chair or two (page 59). Lastly, it is possible to take the modular approach to an extreme, with stackable elements that can be rearranged into tables of different heights, seating, storage, and architectural dividers. In a truly small space, this sort of system could provide a central design theme, while fulfilling several major functions.

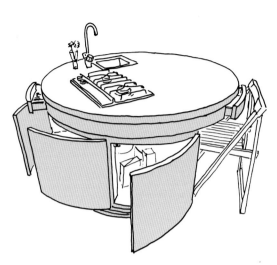

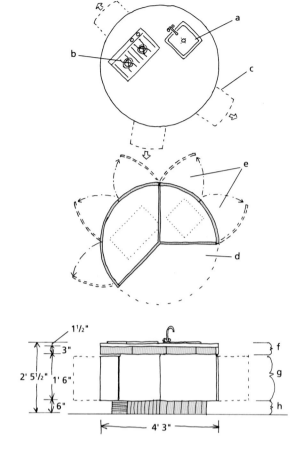

Figs 2a–d. *This 4' 3" diameter kitchen island (photograph on page 59) includes a sink, a double gas burner, three drawers, and ample under-counter storage, and has room for two people to sit and dine comfortably. The only possible improvement would be if it were movable! The components are: **a)** sink, **b)** gas burners, **c)** drawers, **d)** open for legs when seated, **e)** five curved doors, **f)** countertop section, **g)** storage section, **h)** recessed kickplate.*

Figs 3a–b. *American-style futon (mat and frame fold down for sleeping).*

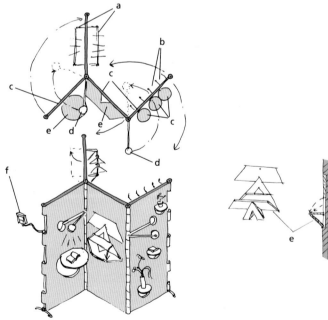

Figs 4a–c. *Multiple folding screen.*
*This screen is fully expandable and modular; new units can be added. The components are: **a)** hanger bars hinge up, lock in position, **b)** clothes hooks swing flat, **c)** mirrors on these faces, **d)** light fixtures swing through openings in screen, **e)** shelves fold out, **f)** miniature TV.*

CHAPTER 13

JUST FOR KITCHENS

K itchens are, well, special. What with their spills, smell, noise, and clutter, it's no wonder cooking areas have traditionally been placed well apart from living quarters whenever possible. On the other hand, cooking is a source of heat, offers an opportunity to chat, and, let's face it, is the ritual which precedes our sustenance—all good reasons to keep the kitchen as close to the center of the home as possible. In fact, it can become the focal point.

Not surprisingly, many of the ideas so far covered in this book have been applied to the particular needs of kitchens. With their need for storage of a bewildering variety of objects and appliances of all shapes, the need for keeping some things cold and others hot, the need for smooth flow of water and fumes, and for accommodating humans moving while holding dangerously hot, sharp, or caustic materials, kitchens pose quite a few problems. And yet, cooking itself is changing, becoming in some ways less messy.

Some Japanese kitchen designers have recognized emerging trends and have directed their attention towards the development of "new" kitchens. On the one hand, the needs of the single dweller have been increasingly well met with small, compact kitchen units which trade refrigerator and stovetop space for speed and convenience (many such minikitchens are sold like appliances, as units with options); some are completely self-enclosed and can be shut out of sight. At the same time, in Japan, for instance, the market has been flooded with compact appliances—tall, skinny refrigerators, tiny heating surfaces, electric bread bakers, coffee makers, microwaves, and hot-water pots, all smaller than ever thought possible, and most of which actually work.

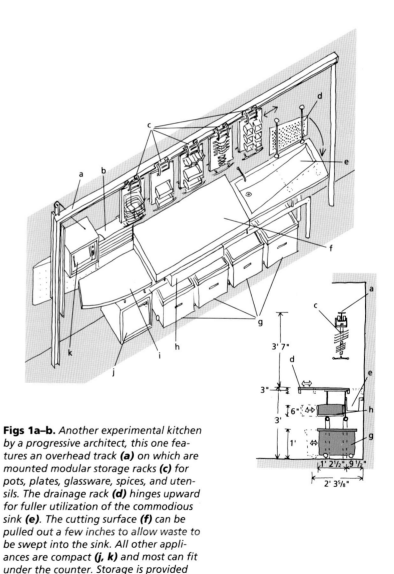

Figs 1a–b. *Another experimental kitchen by a progressive architect, this one features an overhead track (**a**) on which are mounted modular storage racks (**c**) for pots, plates, glassware, spices, and utensils. The drainage rack (**d**) hinges upward for fuller utilization of the commodious sink (**e**). The cutting surface (**f**) can be pulled out a few inches to allow waste to be swept into the sink. All other appliances are compact (**j, k**) and most can fit under the counter. Storage is provided by a set of generic translucent plastic boxes on rollers (**g**). A drawer (**h**), an exhaust hood (**b**), and a secondary ceramic cutting surface (**i**) complete the setup.*

51. The designers of this house, call this a "performance kitchen," and it really is an integral part of the dining space. An open, compact, U-shaped island, it allows the chef to face his or her guests while tossing fettuccine or stir-frying. Slightly unconventional overhead racks provide hanging space for implements, while very simple round shelves keep the saucepans close at hand. The whole is surmounted by a heavy-duty exhaust hood. (By Ushida-Findlay Partnership)

Fig 2. Compact kitchen: **a)** island, **b)** gas range top, **c)** Dutch oven (portable), **d)** drawers, shelves all around base of island, **e)** oven, **f)** dish cabinets, **g)** sink, **h)** storage cabinets, **i)** curved beam (suspended from beams above) holds hanging utensils, **j)** exhaust hood (removed for clarity), **k)** spice rack, **l)** shelves above, cabinet below, **m)** saucepans mounted on vertical post.

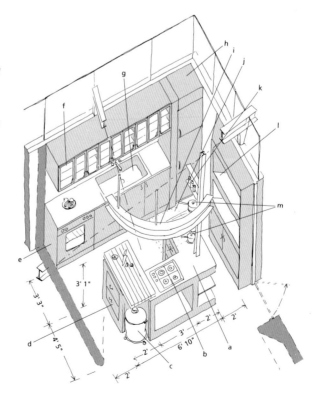

52, 53. This is an experimental kitchen designed by small-space expert Tsuneo Shimojima of Pittori Piccoli for his own home. Noticing that he and his wife rarely ate full meals together at home, Mr. Shimojima set out to create a minimal kitchen fully usable by one person at a time in a space that measures 7' 3" by 4' 3". At the same time, he designed a new type of refrigerator, somewhat along the lines of a convenience store refrigerated showcase, with windows, which could be filled with half-prepared meals organized by day. These could then be put together quickly and simply in this kitchen. In addition to the rounded, human-scaled countertop, special features include removable bowls for ingredients set flush with the surface, allowing cutting boards and other kitchen objects to be firmly placed on top; a wall-mounted coffee maker; a single round sink; a compact but powerful gas burner; and two electric coils. A compact refrigerator supplements the glass-doored one, and, believe it or not, room was found for a dishwasher! All dishes and pots are within easy reach, and, amazingly, the room is filled with natural light and breezes (see fig. 2).

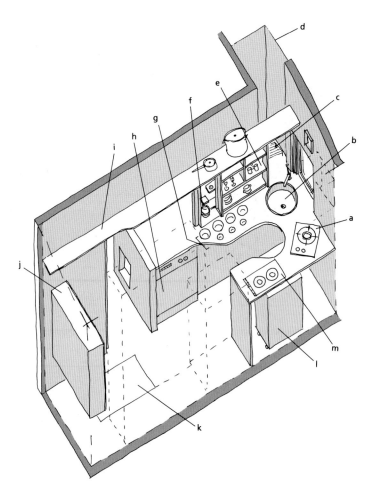

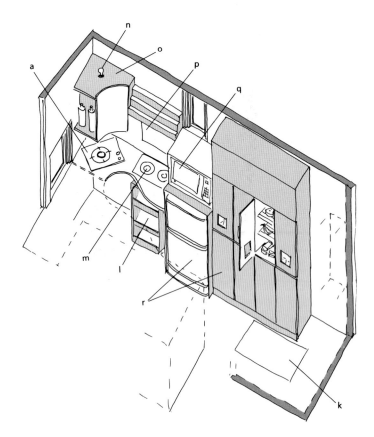

Figs 3a–b. *In this compact kitchen everything is within reach from the central position: **a)** gas burner, **b)** sink, **c)** dish drying rack, **d)** window box, **e)** shelves for dishes, **f)** coffee maker, **g)** removable bowls, **h)** dishwasher, **i)** overhead shelf, **j)** cabinet, **k)** trapdoor to cellar storage, **l)** storage box, **m)** electric cooking elements, **n)** light, **o)** exhaust hood with shelf, **p)** cabinet, **q)** microwave, **r)** refrigerators.*

Then there is the fact that food preparation today now requires almost as much time and space for opening packages as it does for mixing and cooking. Most of us think nothing of eating certain kinds of food out of the container it was bought in. In the case of ready-made microwave meals, the package is often the cookpot and serving dish as well. Then there are deli foods and others which are bought already prepared. Needless to say, the disposal of packaging material requires more space than ever before, despite the efforts of ecologists.

Finally, cooking as a hobby has more and more adherents the world over, and seems to have lost whatever gender-specificity it once had. Cooking for guests can be an important form of recreation and, as in the old days, an opportunity to talk. Accommodating these needs attractively in limited space requires thought and imagination as well.

CHAPTER 14

JUST FOR BATHROOMS

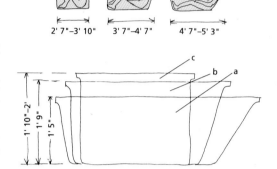

The bathroom is another difficult space, subject to constant technological improvement, which can rarely be called "comfortable." Different cultures have different customs concerning the use of baths and toilets, of course, and they can often be considered together, since so much of the plumbing can serve both. Nevertheless, especially where space is at a premium, it may be wise to separate them physically, if not conceptually.

The degree of privacy one desires is of the greatest importance. That total privacy is important for the toilet area seems to go without saying, but a partially exposed bathtub might be accept-

Fig 1. Bathtub sizes: **a)** western type—takes up the most floor space, **b)** medium sized—not as long as western type, but deeper, **c)** deep, short, traditional Japanese type—takes up least floor space.

Figs 2a–b. Square tub set into floor versus square tub set on top of floor.

Figs 3, 4. Unit bath variations. The "unit bath" is a Japanese invention, now quite common, in which all necessary bath and toilet fixtures are molded in place in prefabricated plastic and fiberglass. For the most part they are economically and functionally sound, and take up a minimum of space. Several manufacturers specialize in these room-sized fixtures, and the current variety of available types is bewildering: with or without toilets, with windows, with built-in water heaters, shower-only. The unit bath is hard to replicate without industrial facilities, but a number of its features—including allocation of space and placement of fixtures—offer valuable hints for those with constricted bathroom space.

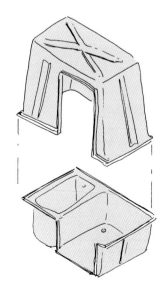

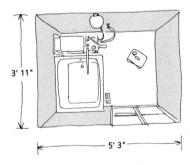
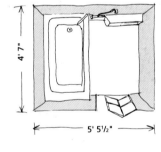
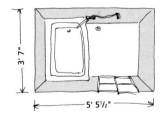
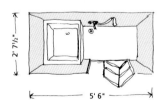

Fig 3. Typical two-piece fiberglass shell construction of unit bath.

Figs 4a–d. Variations on unit bath types (shower used outside tub, drain in floor).

Fig 4a. Small square-tub type with compact water heater; no toilet.
Fig 4b. Large tub with built-in cabinet; no toilet.
Fig 4c. Midsize tub, no toilet.
Fig 4d. Small square-tub type, external water heater.

54. This bath designed for the house "Echo Chamber" (see previous chapter) is actually much smaller than it seems, and is quite snug by western standards. The round shape is generated by the continuous curved wall which defines most of the home, and the generous window opens onto an outdoor pool set in one corner of an enclosed courtyard. In this case, the designers admit to having splurged space on the generous tub—easily big enough for two—partially considering it a communal area, and eliminating more formal communal space instead. Even when the window shades are open, the bath is still private in the sense of being sheltered from outside view; the courtyard itself is fully private (see general introduction, plate 2). (By Ushida-Findlay Partnership)

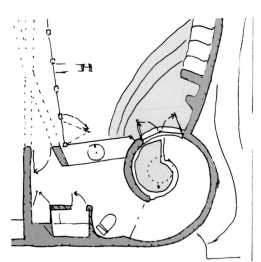

Fig 5.

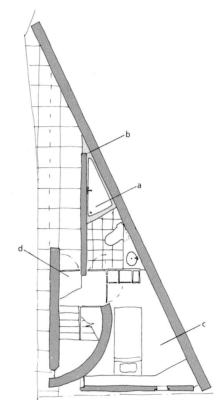

55. One of the ways architect Kiyoshi Sey Takeyama made livable space above a narrow triangular plot of land was to place the bathroom in the most acute corner. Realizing that the foot end of the bathtub needn't be as wide as the back, Takeyama completed the ensemble simply and directly. In this case, the primary building material is reinforced concrete, which lends itself to this kind of form. A narrow vertical window admits a dramatic narrow shaft of light. (By Amorphe Associates)

Figs 6. Triangular bath on the first floor of this unusual three-story triangular house: **a)** bath, **b)** narrow window, **c)** bedroom, **d)** entrance.

able to some (see plates 14, 15). Or the difficult-to-move fixtures may be integrated into the permanent decor with flexible partitions for the few minutes each day when they are in use. Conversely, there may be ways to conceal the toilet when it is not in use while maintaining privacy when it is.

At any rate, the space-expanding ideas discussed so far can be applied to these areas as well. Too few bathrooms really have adequate natural light, for instance, and too few include greenery. Opportunities for rationalizing, compact-ing, and improving hygiene-related storage abound also. Admittedly, both the bath and the toilet are heavily dependent upon available fixtures, but here great strides are being made, with more compact water- and energy-efficient hygienic appliances being developed yearly.

Lastly, there are designs suggested by the limitations of quirkily shaped plots, by floor levels, by affordable materials. The bathroom needn't be fully enclosed, needn't be large, needn't even be permanent. But it should, probably, feel clean.

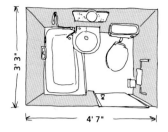

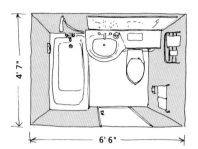

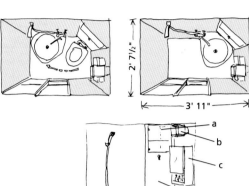

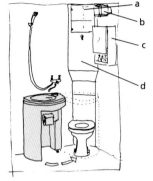

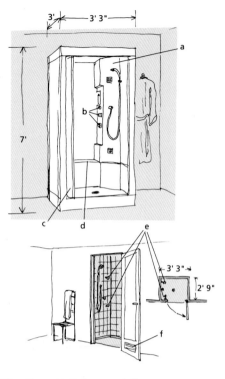

Figs 7a–b. *Two unit bathrooms with tubs, toilets, and sinks. The larger space has a large bath and a counter that extends over the toilet to save room in the smaller room, the toilet has been angled inward.*

Figs 8a–c. *Another type of unit bath allows for a toilet, sink, and shower in approximately 10 square feet. The shower nozzle hangs over the sink. To shower, the sink is swung to the right over the toilet. Other amenities include: **a)** cabinet, **b)** waterproof light fixture, **c)** cabinet with mirror, **d)** toilet tank, water-heater housing.*

Figs 9a–c. *Unit shower stalls. These recent developments with built-in water heaters, lighting, exhaust, and so on, offer some interesting ideas; some are equipped with sauna features. Very well styled and finished outside, they would seem only a little incongruous in most apartments.*
PHONE BOOTH TYPE:
a) water-heater housing, etc.,
b) controls, *c)* door, *d)* seat.
CLOSET TYPE:
e) multiple nozzles, *f)* vent in door.

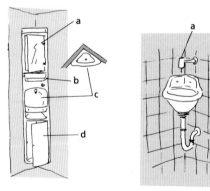

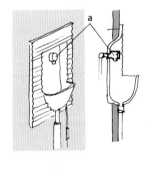

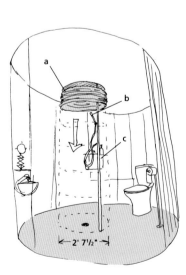

Figs 10a–e. *Space-saving Japanese fixtures.*

Fig 10a. *Typical toilet which uses refill water for washing hands.*
Fig 10b. *Same as figure 10a, with space-saving corner tank.*
Fig 10c. *Corner-mounted lavatory with mirror (a), shelf (b), basin (c), and cabinet (d).*
Fig 10d. *Extra-small corner basin with plunger-type faucet (a).*
Fig 10e. *New recessed ("flush-mount") basin with faucet (a).*

Fig 11. *Collapsible shower stall. This shower stall is adaptable to different situations, here shown as part of a bathroom area with toilet and sink. It can also be installed in the middle of the room, provided a suitable floor and drainage are installed. The curtain (a), made of vinyl with stiffening rings, accordions down from the ceiling. All water and mechanicals are similarly run through the ceiling. Here, a thin vertical rod is provided for mounting the shower nozzle (b)—which can also be made retractable. A shelf (c) for soap, shampoo, and other accessories, stands at the back.*

CHAPTER 15

JUST FOR CHILDREN

As we all know, children's needs differ slightly from adults'. Basically, of course, children can share and use the same rooms, furniture, and facilities as adults, but scale, safety, and what can be described as "friendliness" need to be taken into account. More than this, children need their own spaces. It is no exaggeration to say that security, dignity, and the child's sense of empowerment can be reinforced by architectural gestures. A room of one's own is an understandable, if not always attainable, goal; at least the average child might have his or her own bed.

At the same time, it's nice for children to have an area in which they can play freely, at least at certain times. This is especially true when there is more than one child in the house. In such cases, it may be possible to set off a "children's zone," which features private sleeping areas—small, even bunk-bed-sized, will do—as well as a "communal" play space for which the children will be responsible. Ideally, this play zone should be separate enough from the other rooms that noise and rambunctiousness don't interfere with the other occupants' activities, but are linked closely enough for adult monitoring.

While many can afford private rooms for their children, this is sometimes still a luxury, especially in cities (a recent Japanese television broadcast showed a Tokyo teenager explaining his delinquency by the fact that he shared a room with his elder sister, in bunk beds, the same room serving as a closet for his parents!). But the spatial constraints encountered everywhere sometimes lead to inspired solutions.

Again, the techniques of soft division, level change, and three-dimensionally envisioned storage can be very helpful. Fortunately, childrens'

bodies are small, so clearances can be tighter. In fact, most children prefer nestlike spaces. Also, children's sense of adventure can be stimulated by designs which adults might find merely inconvenient. Above all, the child's space should be flexible enough to adapt to changing abilities, tastes, needs, and limb sizes.

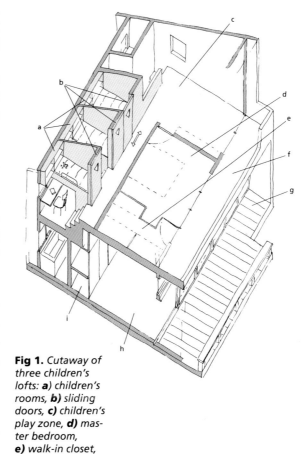

Fig 1. *Cutaway of three children's lofts: **a)** children's rooms, **b)** sliding doors, **c)** children's play zone, **d)** master bedroom, **e)** walk-in closet, **f)** balcony, **g)** terrace, **h)** living, dining, etc., on first floor, **i)** bath.*

56. This is an example of transforming a technical problem into a springboard for something special. This house was well-sited to take advantage of a southern exposure. Because of this, the architect and clients found lots of glass and a high ceiling in the main living area attractive. But how to maintain a more comfortably scaled height in the smaller rooms to the north? The result is this series of three intimately scaled, split-level children's bedrooms, whose matching sliding doors open onto a shared hallway. Entering the loft beds requires a small step up from the entryway; one descends the stairs to use the desk or for access to the clothes storage under the bed. Shelves for books and so on line one wall. Light is admitted through individual skylights and small windows at desk height. A larger room at the top of the stairs serves as a joint play area and opens onto the balcony (see fig. 1). (By Mariko Kimura)

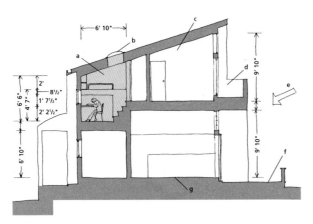

Fig 2. *Side view:* ***a)*** *child's room,* ***b)*** *skylight,* ***c)*** *master bedroom,* ***d)*** *balcony,* ***e)*** *direction of sunlight,* ***f)*** *terrace,* ***g)*** *living/dining.*

57. As can be seen in this shot, the second-floor loft—intended as a child's room or a workroom—further utilizes level change. Here, a small matted nook for sleeping or relaxing is set a few inches above the rest of the floor. (By Atelier Mobile)

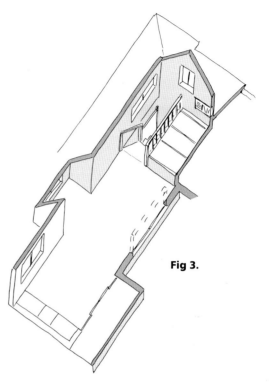

Fig 3.

58. These children's beds take the "trundle bed" idea to a higher level of sophistication. Both beds can be concealed completely, and either can be used separately as well. Beds, desks, closets, and other storage are completely integrated into a clean, harmonious design; the surface in front of the closets is sturdy enough to be stood on for access to high cabinets. Recessed handpulls provide a firm grip but won't catch on clothing (see fig. 4). (By Pittori Piccoli)

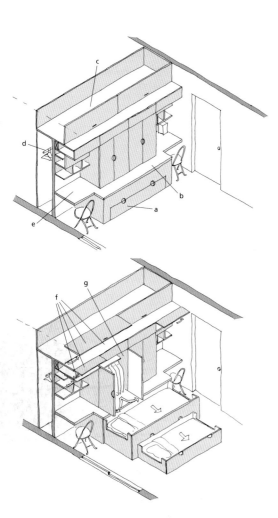

Figs 4a–b. Room with hidden beds and closets:
a) beds pull out, **b)** shelf can be stood on,
c) storage for blankets, etc., **d)** closet for room
on opposite side, **e)** desk surface, **f)** doors
hinge upward, **g)** closet.

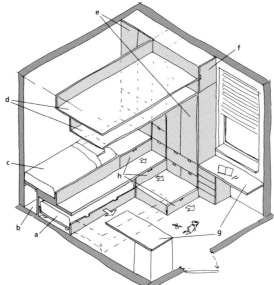

Fig 5. Room for two children.
This room also uses levels, both to define spaces for each
child and to organize storage: **a)** lower bunk pulls out,
b) concealed storage under bunk, **c)** upper bunk, **d)** overhead storage helps define sleeping area, **e)** closets, etc.,
f) cabinet, **g)** desks, **h)** drawers.

Figs 6a–b. Rooms for two children.
These rooms are connected, and interpenetrating in a sense, but still
separate. The window joining the rooms enhances the sense of a
"children's realm," and could probably go in other locations as well.

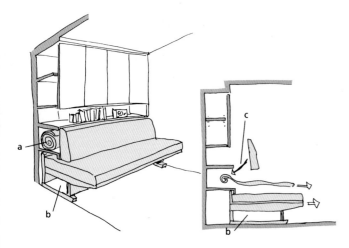

Fig 7. Pull-out bed.
This simple device includes: **a)** bedclothes
storage, **b)** storage space, **c)** bolster fits in
here while bed is in use.

Fig 8. Raised play floor.
This play area is adjacent to the living/dining room and visible
from the kitchen, so children's play can be supervised. The area
features expansive windows, low drawers and cabinets on all
sides for toys, books, and other children's things, and can also
be used as a guest room or whatever when necessary.

JAPANESE HOUSING PAST, PRESENT, AND FUTURE

The history of housing in the world is one marked by evolution, cross-fertilization, stratification, and responsive adaptation to changing climactic and economic circumstances. In this process, technology plays an important role, both as facilitator of innovation and symbol of status and power; more importantly, perhaps, it is technology which has increasingly made possible the exchange of ideas and imagery on a global scale. Global society has always been unified in a sense, through often far-flung trade routes, shared languages, and common roots, but has usually been marked by clearly discernible lobes characterized alternately by relative isolation and by relative freedom of exchange. Japan and the west, particularly America, have for some decades profoundly affected each other's lifestyles through the exchange of dreams, ideals, and technological capabilities; that they will continue to do so is an underlying premise of this book. And yet, as stated in the introduction, though the ideas presented here were all found in Japan, and were chosen for how well they illustrated one or more of the dominant current home-design concepts there, this does not mean they bear an exclusively Asian provenance. It should be clear that nearly all demonstrate strong western influence; this is simply the reality of life in Japan today. That the living conditions of many westerners, particularly in the denser urban areas, will, in the near future, make the adoption of some of the more ingenious current Japanese approaches to living in small spaces increasingly attractive —if not outright necessary—is a thesis which underlies this book.

With about 1,300 years of recorded history, and over 2,000 years of a largely ethnically defined nationhood and culture, Japan has had a long time to develop housing appropriate to the natural situation of the archipelago which it occupies. And yet there is not one, but several lines of development, or traditions, which over the centuries led to a surprising diversity of housing types. On the one hand, these types of houses can be categorized by their origins, that is, as derived from continental Asian or Pacific prototypes, or aboriginal architectural styles. Furthermore, they can be grouped according to the region of Japan in which they are found. Lastly, like most cultures, Japan has always had different types of houses for different classes of people. Add to these elements a particularly energetic penchant for mixture and hybridization, not to mention a strong fashion sense even in the earliest eras, and one is hard-pressed to say with certainty exactly what a "Japanese" house is.

The greatest diversity of architecture in general and houses in particular was, arguably, found in the Japan of the Edo era, which lasted roughly from 1600 to 1868, when the nation was forced out of isolation and into the industrial age. During the Edo period, as now, the form and quality of houses were largely defined by political power. Sumptuary laws, which decreed the number and size of rooms, size and structure of gates, design of windows, size and type of garden, quality and motif of decoration, and roofing materials legally acceptable for members of different social rank (not to mention allowable clothing, furniture, and food), were quite influential. True, many of these laws were honored in the breach, particularly by wealthy merchants who consistently found ways to live like samurai, who were their social, if not always economic, superiors. Political forces also affected the nation's economy, partly through restrictions on mobility and exchange, leading to famine and impoverishment in some parts of the country while others enjoyed relative prosperity, and also imposed limits on technological development, not least through preventing contact with the outside world.

The homes of the elite of this period—the warlords and wealthy samurai—were often quite huge and opulent in their decoration, and yet very conservative, as they adhered to forms and styles codified during earlier centuries when these classes ascended to power. Generally speaking, vast, horizontal one-story villas were the rule, filled with painted screens, elaborate carvings, and copious gold leaf. Like the homes of the ruling classes anywhere, these were not so much places to live as the seats of large economic enterprises, with considerable attention given to security, the reception of guests and supplicants, and the control of servants and retainers. Many notable homes of this type still exist, and have always exerted a strong influence on the lifestyle aspirations of the lower classes. Farmhouses, on the other hand, while often quite large by current standards, with hefty columns, beams, and other structural members

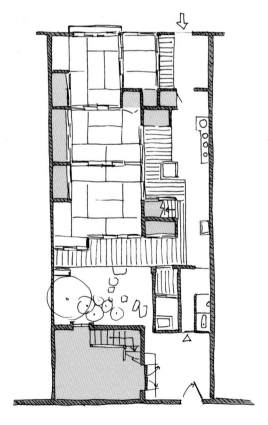

Fig 1. Traditional Japanese house storage zones, townhouse type (shaded areas indicate storage):
a) main entry.
DIRT-FLOORED AREAS:
b) foyer (genkan),
c) kitchen (daidokoro),
d) bath, toilet, **e)** service yard, **f)** garden.
RAISED-FLOOR AREAS:
g) fireproof storehouse,
h) veranda, **i)** alcove,
j) living/sleeping (8 mats),
k) closets, **l)** eating
(6 mats), **m)** reception
(6 mats), **n)** anteroom
(3 mats).

were, like the homes of most of the lower orders, rather plain in their adornment. Unfinished wood surfaces and simple gateways were the rule, and even in the case of large multistory structures, a virtue was made of practicality and humility. Still, these houses had flair, largely due to the ways in which the structural elements themselves were milked for every ounce of expressive power and individuality. Then, as now, wastage was not only economically costly, it was felt unethical and therefore ugly. The same held true for the townhouses of the merchants, who emerged as a powerful class providing services to the aristocracy, during the Muromachi period (1338–1573). Largely due to the crowded conditions of the cities (Edo, now Tokyo, already had one million inhabitants by the mid-eighteenth century), most merchants could not afford to occupy large parcels of ground. Multistory houses, with shops filling most of the ground floor, were quite common, though many had room enough for small gardens in the back, as well as storehouses and other outbuildings (see fig. 1). Although compared with the urban villas of the elite, and even when their owners risked arrest by showing off, merchant houses (*machiya*) today appear quite frugal. When compared with the rowhouse tenements (*nagaya*) occupied by the working classes, they were virtual palaces. The sorry urban living conditions described by mid-nineteenth century western visitors to Japan were not owing to flaws in the architectural design of the residences of the era, but were the direct result of poverty and economic inequality, legacies of a precariously top-heavy political structure.

Much of the poverty and inadequate living conditions suffered by the urban working classes were alleviated, though slowly, following the Meiji Restoration in 1868 and the return to (eventually constitutional) Imperial rule. Careful financial and industrial policy, through selective adoption of western methods, had by the end of the nineteenth century turned Japan into the most modern nation in Asia, and one with a comparably high standard of living. In the case of lifestyle and furnishings, industrialization brought the necessities within reach of nearly the entire populace, and affluence supported the flowering of furniture craft, particularly of *tansu* chests, in most regions of the country, resulting in unprecedented diversity and technical virtuosity while maintaining a traditional look and feel.

In retrospect, of course, it is painfully evident that the westernization/modernization drive was carried to excess during this early period. Much that was unique and precious was either discarded outright or died through neglect, and the most thoroughly modern aspect of the society—the military—was allowed unbridled growth and ambition. The westernization of the Japanese home began with tentative experiments during the last decades of the nineteenth century, often in the form of designs by western architects invited to Japan as teachers. Also, the houses built for foreigners in towns like Yokohama, Nagasaki, Hakodate, and Kobe—the first areas open to foreign residents in the country—though built by local carpenters, provided living examples of these new, alien house forms. Many of these early "western" designs were in fact skilful and handsome hybrids which have in some respects never been surpassed in the harmony with which Japanese and western elements were combined without losing their integrity. For the most part, during the Meiji period (1868–1912), the freedom to play with western-style living belonged only to the elite classes—government officials and wealthy industrialists (then, as now, often one and the same)—whose positions required them to be able to entertain important western guests without embarrassment. Most of these homes, like those of the elite of the preceding generation, were quite large, literally mansions. By the end of World War I, however, westernization in the form of *Bunka Jutaku*, or "Culture Homes," had reached the middle classes as well.

These houses, which were prominently displayed in the media of the time, embodied western features such as dining tables and chairs and modern kitchens, while retaining some rooms which bore an essentially Japanese character. This trend increased with the introduction of apartment-living in the 1920s.

So, then, at least since the end of the Meiji period, and especially in Tokyo, the Japanese living space has been characterized by a blend of traditional and western design. The exact balance of the mix generally depends upon the desires of the homeowner. As early as the 1920s, some Japanese—a fashionable minority—were experimenting with completely cosmopolitan, westernized lifestyles, while their neighbors might still have been living in a manner essentially unchanged since the Edo period. Similarly, today, though the majority of the people are using tables and chairs and perhaps dreaming of owning a home with a front door and a knocker, one can still find families, and even entire communities, who cling to the living patterns of their heritage. However, it is these preservers who are in the minority now. Particularly since the end of World War II, the trend towards western-style—particularly American—living has mushroomed. Part of the reason is that, for most Japanese, "American-style" living and "modern" living are synonymous; it can also be attributed to the deluge of attractive images of American homes which began to wash over a nearly possessionless Japan in 1945. But these factors alone would not have had such a great effect if Japanese people themselves, visiting western-style homes in Japan or overseas and experiencing them firsthand, had not found them warmer, dryer, easier to clean, and generally sturdier and more comfortable than the traditional Japanese type. Although certain technological advances—such as insulation, heating, and well-sealing sliding doors—have recently made equally comfortable and convenient Japanese-style homes possible, even such a modern "traditional" home will appeal only to a few. The traditional home is associated in most contemporary Japanese minds with "oldness": darkness, dinginess, dustiness, and insects in the tatami. In present-day Japan, "old" means "bad." The western-style house is "new" and hence, "good." And besides, it is possible to have a nice new home which is basically western in comfort and atmosphere, but which still has one or two Japanese-style rooms and other accommodations that have surviving uses in the home (fig. 2). At any rate, the "American Dream Home," with a living room, dining room, kitchen, and children's room, suited the post-war rise of the Japanese nuclear family, and became attainable. At the same time, the post-war trend was towards smaller dwellings and rapid urbanization. The degree of westernization in the post-war Japanese home can partly be indicated by the fact that as of 1983, over 65% of households there had dining sets—that is, dining tables and chairs—nearly 50% had western-style beds, and over 40% had the combination of a sofa, armchairs, and a coffee table.

Yet, perhaps the historical underpinnings of some of the Japanese-derived home-design techniques discussed in this book deserve further atten-

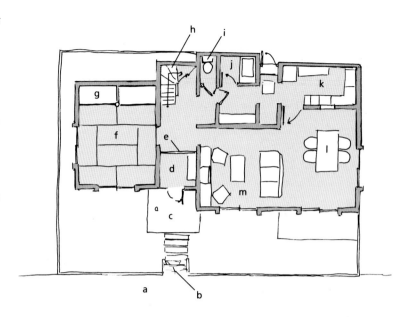

Fig 2. Contemporary Japanese house zones: **a)** street—public, **b)** gate—marks boundary between public and semiprivate, **c)** veranda—semiprivate, **d)** entranceway (genkan)—indoors, but still semiprivate; shoes can be worn to this point, **e)** step up—marks boundary between semiprivate and private; indoor slippers provided by occupants for guests to use beyond this point, **f)** Japanese-style room—most formal room; only stockinged feet allowed; generally not entered unless invited, **g)** alcove (tokonoma) for decorative display, **h)** stairs to bedroom above—very private, **i)** toilet—special slippers provided; entering with slippers used in rest of house is the greatest social taboo, **j)** bath—very private; only bare feet allowed, **k)** kitchen—usually not freely entered by guests, **l)** dining area, **m)** living area—sofa, armchairs, coffee table, television.

tion. A good place to start would be with the issue of horizontality.

As mentioned above, with the notable exception of the castles which began to be constructed throughout the country in the mid-sixteenth century (under the influence of the first western missionaries and builders to visit the country), Japanese homes, even those of the elite, tended to be of one story, expanding in several directions horizontally. In fact, houses of two or more stories were, until the Meiji period, generally found only in colder rural areas, such as the mountains of Gifu prefecture (where the snow regularly becomes so deep that the main entrances were built on the second floor), and in the denser urban areas. The reasons for this are still being debated, but they seem to be primarily climatic and technical. For one, the winters of most of the archipelago, especially the southern regions which were settled earliest and from which most later housing types were derived, are relatively mild, while the summers can be unbearably hot. So, while a variety of limited measures were developed for dealing with the cold—including heavily quilted clothing, small portable braziers, and sheer endurance—most aspects of house design were geared towards increasing comfort during the summer months. Whereas the earliest Japanese houses were so-called "pit dwellings," built half-sunken into the earth, during the Kofun period (300–710), the powerful Yamato clan began living in raised floor

dwellings (most Japanese, however, continued to use pit dwellings, which were still seen as late as the sixteenth century). The raised house, like those found on many islands in the Pacific, eventually became the dominant type, however; the design allows breezes to pass underneath, and, coupled with the widely overhanging eaves and fully openable exterior walls, optimized ventilation and natural cooling.

Although chairs, brought at first from China and later from Europe, enjoyed brief decades of popularity as expensive toys for the elite, Japan is unique in the degree to which its entire domestic architecture adapted itself to the low viewpoint dictated by floor-sitting. Although cushions and specialized seating appliances—such as portable arm rests—were developed, the greatest single adaptation was to make the entire floor a soft, resilient surface suitable for sitting or reclining. The now well-known *tatami* mat, which remains characteristic of Japanese living space, first appeared as a portable item, primarily for sleeping, for which it was set atop a raised wooden frame, in the eighth century; by the fourteenth century it had evolved into the full-floor covering we know today.

The types of furnishings appropriate for floor-living need to be, of course, lightweight, low, and movable—and kept to the minimum. Of course, over the course of a thousand years these items have undergone considerable evolution, but can broadly be divided into items for eating, sleeping,

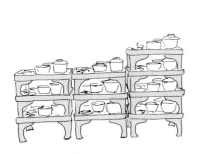

Fig 3. *Modular tray-tables: These tray-tables, called* zen, *are designed to allow meals for several persons to be entirely prepared and served in the kitchen, brought in in stacks, and set before the guests. Many varieties exist; this particular style is called* Sowa-zen, *and is said to have been designed by tea master Kanamori Sowa in the early seventeenth century.*

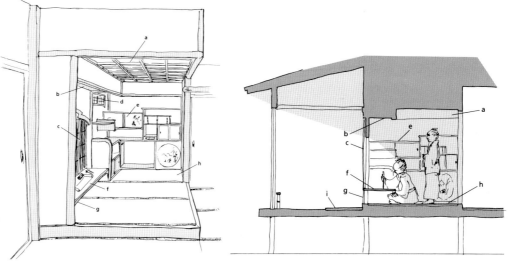

Figs 4a–b. *Study nook of Katsura Palace, Kyoto (seventeenth century): a) ceiling over nook is lower than those of surrounding rooms, b) lowermost ceiling over desk, c) upper window closed with* shoji *screens for diffused light; opened for view of garden outside, d) small window, e) shelving units, f) desk, g) low window lets light in under desk, h) raised floor area, i) veranda.*

writing, and storage—often of eating, sleeping, and writing implements. Also, items designed for dressing and applying cosmetics should be included.

Until the modern period, there were no fixed tables for dining. Rather, people of all classes ate from small portable tables, often more like legged trays. These were usually made stackable (see fig. 3), and could be arranged on the floor in a variety of configurations as situations demanded. Of course, they were used while seated on low floor cushions (*zabuton*). A hybrid Japanese/western dining table, the *chabudai*, appeared after World War I. It was big enough to hold everyone's dishes at once, as in the west, but built low to accommodate floor-sitting. The *chabudai* continues to be widely used today.

Layers of quilts called *futon* laid on top of *tatami* mats were the only sleeping furniture known until the modern period, with the exception of the early Imperial raised bed frames mentioned earlier. Comfortable, good for the spine, and easy to store, the *futon*, in modified form, is enjoying increasing popularity in the west (see page 76, fig. 3), even as more and more Japanese turn to western beds. As mentioned earlier, the use of the *futon* spurred the development of specialized deep, wide storage cabinets and closets (see page 60, fig. 1). Until this century, it was used with high, hard pillows designed to preserve carefully arranged hairstyles, and which were more like furniture than bedding (see general introduction, fig. 7).

Small portable desks—often lavishly decorated in lacquer and gold—and special cabinets to hold boxed writing implements and books appeared very early on and were used until the modern period, and, in limited cases, until today. These were often accompanied by padded, portable arm rests. All were, of course, taken out only when needed. However, during the fifteenth century, desks began to be built into special windowed alcoves called *shoin* (see fig. 4); this trend began in temples, where monks often needed to spend days on end in study, and soon spread to the educated classes. The *shoin*, which included fixed decorated shelves as well, eventually spawned the *tokonoma* alcove, used exclusively for display (see figs. 1, 2; general introduction, fig. 6). These can be considered the first Japanese built-in furniture. Also, merchants used special small desks for accounting, often fitted with drawers, safes, abacuses, and other handy fixtures.

Major storage furnishings fall into categories of box-type, drawer-type, and shelf-type. The earliest known items were low lidded chests, often on legs, simple, well-built cabinets with doors, and utilitarian standing open shelves. *Tansu*, the handsomely designed drawered cabinets so well known in the west, are a rather late development; with one or two notable exceptions, drawered furniture didn't come into use until the Edo period (1600–1868). *Tansu* experienced a real boom in the late seventeenth century, however, and evolved into

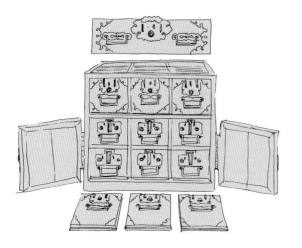

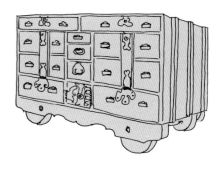

Figs 5a–b. *Sea chests, or* funa dansu, *represent a peak in compactness and modularity. Intended for use on ships, they were very sturdily built and heavily reinforced with iron hardware, with compartments for money, business papers, passports, abacuses, and even stools. This particular one has an upper false-drawer front which removes to expose three individually locking strongbox drawers; the lower cabinet doors open to reveal a set of six similar locking drawers.*

Fig 6. *In Japan, at least, portable wheeled chests, called* kuruma-dansu, *have a venerable ancestry, since they were an early solution to the need for rapid evacuation of valuables during fires and earthquakes.*

numerous specific types for different functions and from different regions (see figs. 5, 6; general introduction, fig. 4). Similarly, the commodious closet depended upon the development of the sliding screen, which didn't appear until the 1400s.

In addition to the sliding screen, room dividers have included folding screens (*byobu*), single-panel standing screens (*tsuitate*), opaque sliding screens (*fusuma*, often painted), translucent sliding screens (*shoji*), translucent hanging bamboo blinds (*misu*, like *sudare* with decorative borders), freestanding curtains (*kicho*), hanging curtains (*tobari*), and draw-type curtains (*hikimono*), often all used together to shape and decorate living space. Indeed, the *shinden*-style dwelling, used by the aristocracy of the tenth to the twelfth centuries, was essentially an open, columned structure whose interior was divided by these types of lightweight items, and whose exterior could be closed by hanging, drop-leaf shutters (*shitomido*) when necessary. It was protected from the rain but otherwise exposed to the weather.

Kitchens, which until the modern era were dirt-floored areas adjacent to the raised living zones, gradually have found their way into the interior of the home proper. This is primarily due to technological advances, largely western in origin, which minimize mess and eliminate smoke. Also, households are not as large as they once were, and no longer need to serve daily meals to a dozen or more people at once, which means kitchens can be smaller. The Japanese kitchen looks pretty much

like its western counterpart (or prototype), yet even now there is always a rice cooker, a large vacuum flask (usually pump-operated) with hot water for making tea, and some sort of grill for fish.

Similarly, bathrooms and toilets have adopted the best of the west while retaining the more comfortable Japanese features. Like the kitchen, they have been brought indoors and raised up to the level of the rest of the home. They are still differentiated by floor surface, and can't be entered either with shoes or the slippers used in the rest of the house (see fig. 2). Unlike the American custom—but like many parts of Europe—the bathtub and the toilet usually have separate rooms, both for privacy and to separate the "clean" tub from the "unclean" toilet. But, as mentioned in the section on bathrooms, space restrictions may override this separation in many instances. The bathtub is usually the traditional short, deep type, and one still finds the traditional wooden one now and then. Toilets have evolved from the pre-modern rectangular hole in the latrine floor to modern porcelain fixtures, about half of which are floor-mounted squat-types, and half western seat-types. They are usually built with a sink on top of the tank so that one can wash one's hands with the water that refills it, saving both space and water (see page 84, fig. 10). Recent years have seen the seat-type develop into an electronic device which automatically washes and drys the user's posterior, and can even take his blood pressure! Their water-saving features are more than offset by Japanese ladies who invariably flush once before starting, to camouflage their own noise, and again when finished; now, however, toilet-paper mounts are being fitted with electronic speakers which emit the sound of rushing water, thus preserving modesty while conserving water.

The Japanese mania for compact, flexible designs was mentioned briefly earlier, but deserves to be elaborated upon. The examples are endless. *Yatai*, for instance, are traditional pushcarts, quite common to this day, serving food, liquor, and nocturnal warmth. The typical *yatai* folds up and into itself for easy transport, but when open for business becomes a comfy small room. Some are quite sophisticated examples of portable architecture (see fig. 7). The *furoshiki* is a simple square of cloth. It perhaps epitomizes compactness and flexibility, because, not only can it be used elegantly to wrap and carry all manner of gifts, from cakes to kimono to payoff money but it is also incredibly strong, practically weightless, and folds into nothingness. Even the traditional *sutra* cabinets found in temples often had to fit into small niches, and so were tall, narrow, and made rotatable so that every scroll could be located and removed easily.

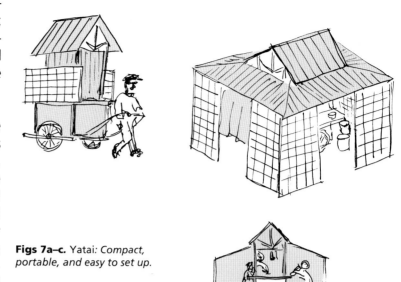

Figs 7a–c. Yatai: *Compact, portable, and easy to set up.*

In contemporary life, almost every item of daily use has been given similar consideration. Hot-water heaters are also usually quite compact, and designed to heat water quickly on demand only, saving gas as well as space. There is a vast variety of compact, efficient heaters on the market here as well, including quartz and infrared, most suitable for heating only one person. Also, since it has been discovered that if one's feet are warm, one's whole body will feel warm, there are many types of small electric area rugs, electric slippers, and electric robes on the market, all of which are in common use. Not to mention wall-mounted air conditioner/heater units (called "central heating" in Japan) which have been getting thinner, lighter, and quieter every year.

Other appliances, such as washing machines, stoves, refrigerators, and microwave ovens are designed with compactness foremost in mind. This goes as far as the manufacture of exceedingly tall and thin refrigerators, ones whose doors open from either direction, and extremely popular ones which fit under counters, ideal for single living. There are also models which fit under the floor. Stereos, of course, are rapidly approaching noth-ingness, and miniature, flat or projected television screens will soon eliminate "the box." Most of these are used worldwide, but they are *needed* in Japan. Finally, Japanese department stores and mail-order catalogs are a storage-freak's dream. The sheer variety and ingenuity of the items available and in common use are astounding. Again, the most interesting designs couple concealed storage with collapsible working surfaces, casters, and modularity. There are hundreds of items made to fit Japanese closets, designed for everything from suits to shoes to sewing machines to rolls of wrapping paper, again all modular, removable, and dustproof (see page 60, fig. 1). There are tall, skinny bookshelves six paperbacks wide and three deep, electric lift jacks that allow you to park one car over the other, and vacuum cleaners the size of handbags. In fact, living spaces themselves have recently been conceived as "compact appliances" as in the now familiar "capsule hotels," and in the new "systems homes" (figs. 8, 9).

In coming decades, more and more people will be able to move to the countryside and commute to work "telelectronically" with increasing use of faxes, modems, and the telephone. But for those of us who need to live in modern cities, either by necessity or inclination, and want to live beautifully and wisely, there will be more and more reason to learn from the Japanese—not the elite, who can still occupy urban villas, but the common people who live within limits and the designers who struggle to answer their needs.

Fig 8. *Capsule hotel: Very common in cities, these accommodations are generally used by businessmen for a single night. Men and women are separated, with dormitory-style bath and toilet facilities. Most capsules are equipped with TV, radio, alarm clock, and so on, with a small shelf for belongings. Lockers are provided for the rest.*

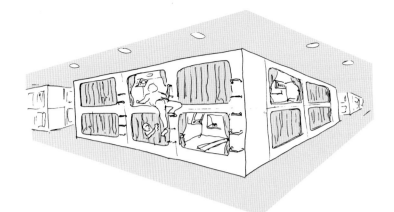

Figs 9a–e. *"System home": This is an entirely modular, prefabricated living unit for one person in under 200 square feet. It features a unit bath (see pages 81–84, figs. 3–8), a bed which rises to the ceiling when not in use (see page 72, fig. 6), fold-out dining table and kitchen, and modular storage cabinets. Amenities include:* **a)** *space bed,* **b)** *entertainment module—TV monitor, audio-visual system, etc.,* **c)** *working module—desk, computer, rotating storage for books, etc., above,* **d)** *dressing module—hanging storage, drawers, etc., for clothing,* **e)** *accessory module—smaller drawers for odds and ends,* **f)** *storage module—larger shelves and cabinets for storage,* **g)** *unit bath module,* **h)** *kitchen module—refrigerator below; swing-out panel above (see detail) with ceramic cooking surface, storage; microwave, sink, etc., in rear,* **i)** *dining module—table folds down, chairs attached, storage for dishes, etc., above,* **j)** *relaxation module—fold-down easy-chair (when bed is raised) with "body-sonic" system, alpha-wave generator, surround speakers; can be used along with entertainment module opposite when bed is in raised position (see detail),* **k)** *air conditioning unit, ceiling storage unit above (not shown).*

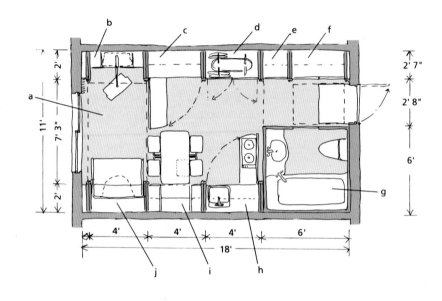

Detail of relaxation module.

Detail of kitchen module.

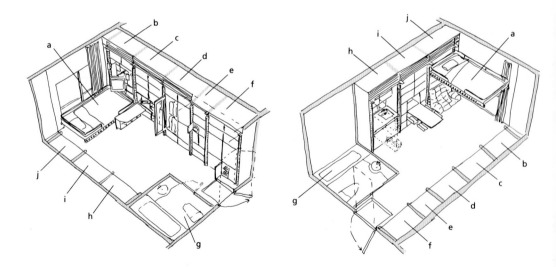